Cambridge Elements

Elements in Philosophy and Logic
edited by
Bradley Armour-Garb
SUNY Albany
Frederick Kroon
The University of Auckland

LOGIC AND SCIENCE

An Exploration of Logical Anti-Exceptionalism

Filippo Ferrari
University of Bologna

Massimiliano Carrara
University of Padua

Shaftesbury Road, Cambridge CB2 8EA, United Kingdom

One Liberty Plaza, 20th Floor, New York, NY 10006, USA

477 Williamstown Road, Port Melbourne, VIC 3207, Australia

314–321, 3rd Floor, Plot 3, Splendor Forum, Jasola District Centre,
New Delhi – 110025, India

103 Penang Road, #05–06/07, Visioncrest Commercial, Singapore 238467

Cambridge University Press is part of Cambridge University Press & Assessment,
a department of the University of Cambridge.

We share the University's mission to contribute to society through the pursuit of
education, learning and research at the highest international levels of excellence.

www.cambridge.org
Information on this title: www.cambridge.org/9781009547819

DOI: 10.1017/9781009233897

© Filippo Ferrari and Massimiliano Carrara 2025

This publication is in copyright. Subject to statutory exception and to the provisions
of relevant collective licensing agreements, with the exception of the Creative
Commons version the link for which is provided below, no reproduction
of any part may take place without the written permission of Cambridge University
Press & Assessment.

An online version of this work is published at doi.org/10.1017/9781009233897 under
a Creative Commons Open Access license CC-BY-NC 4.0 which permits re-use,
distribution and reproduction in any medium for non-commercial purposes providing
appropriate credit to the original work is given and any changes made are indicated.
To view a copy of this license visit https://creativecommons.org/licenses/by-nc/4.0

When citing this work, please include a reference to the DOI 10.1017/9781009233897

First published 2025

A catalogue record for this publication is available from the British Library

ISBN 978-1-009-54781-9 Hardback
ISBN 978-1-009-23390-3 Paperback
ISSN 2516-418X (online)
ISSN 2516-4171 (print)

Cambridge University Press & Assessment has no responsibility for the persistence
or accuracy of URLs for external or third-party internet websites referred to in this
publication and does not guarantee that any content on such websites is, or will
remain, accurate or appropriate.

For EU product safety concerns, contact us at Calle de José Abascal, 56, 1°, 28003
Madrid, Spain, or email eugpsr@cambridge.org

Logic and Science

An Exploration of Logical Anti-Exceptionalism

Elements in Philosophy and Logic

DOI: 10.1017/9781009233897
First published online: April 2025

Filippo Ferrari
University of Bologna

Massimiliano Carrara
University of Padua

Author for correspondence: Filippo Ferrari, f.q.ferrari@gmail.com

Abstract: This Element delves into the relationship between logic and the sciences, a topic brought to prominence by Quine, who regarded logic as methodologically and epistemologically akin to the sciences. For this reason, Quine is seen as the forefather of anti-exceptionalism about logic (AEL), a stance that has become prevalent in the philosophy of logic today. Despite its popularity and the volume of research it inspires, some core issues still lack clarity. For one thing, most works in the debate remain vague on what should count as logic and what should count as a science. Furthermore, the terms of the comparison are rarely specified and discussed in a systematic way. This Element purports to advance the debate on these crucial issues with the hope of fostering our understanding of the fundamentals of AEL. This title is also available as Open Access on Cambridge Core.

Keywords: logic, science, logical anti-exceptionalism, philosophy of logic, demarcation problem in science and logic

© Filippo Ferrari and Massimiliano Carrara 2025

ISBNs: 9781009547819 (HB), 9781009233903 (PB), 9781009233897 (OC)
ISSNs: 2516-418X (online), 2516-4171 (print)

Contents

Introduction	1
1 On Full-Blooded Exceptionalism	2
2 Quine's Philosophy of Logic	18
3 Demarcation in Science	26
4 Demarcation in Logic	36
5 Logic and Science: A Multicriteria Approach	47
Conclusions	63
References	68

Introduction

This Element offers a short philosophical inquiry into the relationship between logic and the sciences. This topic is arguably as old as the discipline of logic itself, which we can date back to Aristotle's syllogistic, the general discipline that studies valid deductive arguments.[1] Although the first known occurrence of the term *logikê* (in the somehow contemporary sense of a discipline on its own) comes from the Stoics,[2] it is standardly assumed, as Gisela Striker points out, that "Aristotle's Prior Analytics marks the beginning of formal logic" (Striker 2009: xi). Throughout the *Analytics*, syllogistics provides a uniform theory of deduction for both assertoric and modal contexts within dialectical and scientific realms. For Aristotle the chief distinction between these realms lies in how premises (definitions) are established. In dialectics, definitions typically govern the use or meaning of terms, while in science, they concern the nature of the definienda (objects, not terms). This also explains why only the conclusions of scientific syllogisms express necessary facts. Therefore, Aristotle's *Analytics* presents an early instance of integrating the general discipline of deductive argument with the practice of scientific demonstration.

In contemporary philosophical discussions about logic, on which this Element will focus, the relationship between logic and the sciences has become a focal point, primarily due to the influence of Quine's works in the philosophy of logic. In fact, Quine, who conceived of logic in continuity with the sciences both from a methodological and an epistemological point of view, is typically considered the forefather of what is nowadays known as anti-exceptionalism about logic (AEL for short). AEL is a prominent position and a prolific movement in contemporary philosophy of logic, grounded in the idea that there is significant continuity between various aspects of the sciences and logic.

Despite its popularity and the fact that a considerable amount of research in the philosophy of logic gravitates around anti-exceptionalist themes, some core issues still lack clarity. Most works in the debate remain vague on what should count as logic and what should count as science. Specifically, the terms of the comparison are rarely specified and discussed in a systematic way. This short Element purports to advance the debate on these crucial issues with the hope of fostering our understanding of the fundamentals of logical anti-exceptionalism. In doing so, our goal is not to advocate for or defend logical

---

[1] Aristotle's logic is known as term-logic since it is about the logical relations between terms, and can be considered as the predecessor of modern predicate-logic. The Stoics, in particular Chrysippus, are credited for the invention of what is nowadays known as propositional logic – see Striker (2009: xiii) and Bobzien (2020) for an introduction to ancient logic. Moreover, Aristotle did not conceive of syllogistic as a science (epistêmê) in its own right.

[2] On this see Diogenes Laertius' *Lives of the Philosophers*, VII 39–41.

anti-exceptionalism – a position on which we intend to remain neutral for the purposes of this Element.

We will proceed as follows. In the first section we provide some preliminary discussion of logical anti-exceptionalism in relation to the question whether and to what extent logic is a science. Specifically, we introduce and compare two ways of understanding logical anti-exceptionalism: (i) in terms of continuity with the sciences, and (ii) in terms of tradition rejection. Then, for dialectical purposes, we lay out a position we label *full-blooded exceptionalism about logic*. We take full-blooded exceptionalism to be a fictional view which nevertheless offers a neat paradigm of a position that exemplifies the various features that recent anti-exceptionalist views have rejected. As it will become clear toward the end of Section 1, the boundary between exceptionalist and anti-exceptionalist positions is not a sharp one, and one could subscribe to an anti-exceptionalist view, for instance, to a greater or lesser degree, depending on which anti-exceptionalist features she endorses.[3] The second section discusses some of the main tenets of Quine's philosophy of logic as a precursor of logical anti-exceptionalism, focusing in particular on his influential criticisms to some traditional categories (such as those of analyticity, necessity, apriority) that have been historically attributed to logic. Sections 3 and 4 deal, respectively, with the issue of demarcation in science and in logic. Although no definite conclusion is reached in terms of how to demarcate science from non-science and logic from non-logic, putting these two debates side by side helps to identify some key elements that are essential for effectively guiding the comparison between logic and science. Relying on these elements, Section 5 provides the groundwork for a more systematic comparison between logic and the sciences and contextually discusses three (for limit of space) prominent proposals within the logical anti-exceptionalism landscape by, respectively, Timothy Williamson, Penelope Maddy, and a joint proposal by Ole Hjortland and Ben Martin. The Element closes with a short conclusion highlighting some of the most prominent and pressing issues for logical anti-exceptionalism.

1 On Full-Blooded Exceptionalism

1.1 The Status of Logic

Sciences such as biology, chemistry, and physics (i.e. what goes ordinarily under the label *natural sciences*),[4] primarily aim to provide us with new insights

---

[3] See, for instance, Sher (2023a). Perhaps Read (2019) also falls under this category.
[4] The emphasis on *natural* sciences is due to the fact that generally within the anti-exceptionalist debate coming from Quine the comparison is between logic (and logical theory) and these sciences (scientific theories about the natural world). There are other ways of understanding the

and explanations about previously unknown phenomena or to offer more comprehensive explanations of already known phenomena. It is, indeed, standard to maintain that through discoveries in these scientific fields, we uncover what are often considered new substantive truths about the world. In other words, the sciences provide us with new and substantive information about certain natural phenomena. What about logic? Is logic akin to the sciences?

Facing this question, one may think that there's some pressure to lean toward a simple affirmative answer to the question: "Is logic a science?" that comes naturally from putting together two prima facie intuitive thoughts: (i) that logic and mathematics are closely linked – in particular, that logic is part of mathematics, and (ii) that mathematics is naturally associated with the sciences. A straightforward way of making the link between logic and mathematics explicit is to consider deductivism in mathematics. As discussed by Maddy (2022: 9), deductivism holds that a mathematical sentence "p" should be understood as asserting the proposition that p can be inferred from a suitable set of axioms through a deductive process. For example, the sentence "$2 + 2 = 4$" is interpreted by proponents of deductivism as stating the proposition that $2 + 2 = 4$ logically follows from the axioms of arithmetic. In this view, logic is an integral part of mathematics, suggesting that if mathematics is a science, then logic should be considered a science as well.

As always in philosophy, things may, of course, not be that simple. Although deductivism offers one specific example, it nevertheless illustrates that there are substantive assumptions that have been made in order to establish the link between logic and the sciences. However, one may have reasons not to accept a particular view of the connection between logic and mathematics – that is, deductivism in our example. Alternatively, one may indeed argue that the association between mathematics and the (natural) sciences is not that straightforward. In fact, whether, and to what extent, mathematics is continuous with the natural sciences is certainly an open and interesting question. In this respect, when it comes to the relationship between logic and the sciences a critical question remains: How significantly does logic resemble sciences like biology, physics, and chemistry?

In contrast with the intuitive link between logic and the sciences via mathematics, in several conceptions logic is seen as markedly different from the

---

term "science" – one may for instance think that logic, perhaps together with mathematics, is a science in some kind of sui generis sense of "science." This wouldn't be a particularly exciting thesis. Be that as it may, we stick with the way in which "science" is understood within the relevant debates in the philosophy of logic. Accordingly, unless specified otherwise, by "sciences" we mean natural sciences. Sections 3 and 4 will be dedicated to a thorough discussion of how to conceive of "science" and how to conceive of "logic."

sciences. First, logic is often taken to provide formal tools that serve as a neutral and impartial arbiter in evaluating scientific and philosophical disputes. Second, logic is often viewed as insensitive to empirical evidence, in terms of both justification and revision. Third, logic is primarily considered a normative discipline, and not a descriptive one which is supposed to be in the business of offering explanations about the world. For instance, logical expressivists claim that since logic has an expressive role – for example, in Brandom's version "to make explicit the inferential relations that articulate the semantic contents of the concepts expressed by the use of ordinary, nonlogical vocabulary" (Brandom 2018: 70) – logical sentences are not representational: they are not meant to make statements about the world and cannot fulfill the function of explaining facts beyond its own realm. In short, conceptions of logic such as logical expressivism see a clear divide between logic and the sciences.

In the philosophy of logic, such a standard divide has been widely discussed. The discussion follows three partially overlapping trends: (i) an epistemological one, where philosophers have focused on whether logic can be justified and/or revised based on empirical evidence; (ii) a methodological one, which particularly addresses whether logical theories should be selected using broadly abductive methods, similar to those employed in selecting scientific theories; (iii) a metaphysical one concerning whether logic's subject matter is about some, perhaps very general and structural, aspects of reality. The complexity of determining whether and to what extent logic is a science requires establishing criteria to demarcate what counts as logic and what counts as science. This important issue will be addressed in Sections 3 and 4.

Before we delve into the discussion about logic's status as a science, it's important to clarify some terminology. In this debate, "logic" is generally used in a restrictive sense, referring specifically to deductive logic rather than to various non-deductive logics like inductive or abductive logic. Throughout this Element, we will adhere to this narrower definition of "logic," focusing primarily on the relationship between deductive logic and the sciences. Furthermore, we will adopt what has been the traditional twentieth-century view of logic as a discipline concerned with reasoning – what Priest refers to as the canonical application of logic (see Priest 2006).[5] Roughly, by logic in the sense of a discipline we mean the interpreted logical theory (or the set of interpreted

---

[5] This may be seen as a limiting assumption, especially for those who are sympathetic to an instrumentalist conception of logic according to which there's a multiplicity of aims and application of our logic(s), none of which is privileged – see, for instance, Commandeur (forthcoming). That being said, we believe that there are quite convincing arguments for thinking that there's some special connection between logic and reasoning – a connection that may suggest something even stronger than reasoning being the canonical application of logic (on this, see Hanna 2009; Boghossian & Wright 2023; Kripke 2023).

logical theories) – that is, in which each logical constant has an intended interpretation – which is (are) accepted and employed by logicians.

1.2 Quine's Philosophy of Logic and the Rise of Logical Anti-Exceptionalism

The question of whether logic should be considered a science has been a recurring theme throughout many historical discussions on the nature of logic, as evidenced in the works of philosophers like Leibniz, Hobbes, Descartes, Kant, Boole, Frege, Husserl, and Russell, among others. However, this question gained sharper focus and more refined treatment following the influential contributions of Bertrand Russell and Willard Van Orman Quine to epistemology and to the philosophy of logic. In some of their writings (e.g., Russell 1918; Quine 1951, 1986a), they contend that logic bears substantial resemblance to the sciences, particularly the natural sciences, based on epistemological, metaphysical, and methodological considerations. As Bertrand Russell famously claimed, "logic is concerned with the real world just as truly as zoology, though with its more abstract and general features" (Russell 1919: 169).

Quine famously took logic to be continuous with the natural sciences. And many prominent philosophers of logic and philosophical logicians currently sympathize with the Quinean thesis that logic, as a discipline, should be considered methodologically and epistemologically akin to the natural sciences.[6] In the fairly recent debate within the philosophy of logic, this thesis is known as anti-exceptionalism about logic. While the label in connection to logic is due to Ole Hjortland (Hjortland 2017), the inspiration for AEL is from the kind of philosophical methodology developed by Timothy Williamson in his book *The Philosophy of Philosophy* (Williamson 2007). Our discussion of AEL will necessarily encompass multiple facets. Indeed AEL challenges the notion that logic's methodology, epistemology, and subject matter possess an exceptional status and advocates for a more intimate amalgamation of logic with the natural sciences. Additionally, AEL posits a parallel connection between the laws of logic and those governing the world, akin to the relationship seen in scientific laws. Lastly, AEL, drawing inspiration from Quine's concept of evidential holism, implies that the justification of logic mirrors the approach used for substantiating scientific theories.

Two broad ways of characterizing AEL have been proposed and discussed in recent works. The first suggests understanding AEL in terms of *continuity* with

---

[6] Prominent anti-exceptionalists are, for instance, Pen Maddy, Gila Sher, Gillian Russell, Tim Williamson, Graham Priest, and Ole Hjortland.

the natural sciences (AEL-as-continuity), while the second casts AEL out in terms of *rejection* of some or all of the characteristics that traditionally have been attributed to logic (AEL-as-tradition-rejection). Let's briefly describe these two ways of understanding AEL.

As the very label suggests, AEL-as-continuity is the thesis that there is a significant continuity between logic and the sciences on a variety of aspects (crucially, as said, on methodological, epistemological, and metaphysical aspects). In his 2017 paper, Ole Hjortland introduced the position precisely in terms of such a *continuity*. In an often-cited passage which is typically used as a sort of AEL-manifesto, Hjortland claims that "Logic isn't special. *Its theories are continuous with science; its method continuous with scientific method.* Logic isn't a priori, nor are its truths analytic truths. Logical theories are revisable, and if they are revised, they are revised on the same grounds as scientific theories" (Hjortland 2017: 631, our italics).

Susane Haack, anticipating by several years the recent anti-exceptionalist trend, claims that "[L]ogic is a theory, a theory on a par, except for its extreme generality, with other, 'scientific' theories; and according to which choice of logic, as of other theories, is to be made on the basis of an assessment of the economy, coherence and simplicity of the overall belief set" (Haack 1974: 26).

The second way of characterizing AEL is in terms of a *rejection* of what may be taken to be the traditional conception of logic which sees logic as having a set of very special features which make logic an exceptional discipline.[7] What are these features? According to the way in which Hjortland and Martin introduce the position in some of their joint works, logic possesses some or most of the following features: it is an *absolutely general*, *purely formal*, and *normative* discipline which deals with *truths* that are both *analytic and necessary*, the justification of which is *non-inferential*, a priori, and *empirically non-revisable*. We may call a conception of logic which endorses all these special characteristics a full-blooded exceptionalist conception. In short, *full-blooded exceptionalism*.[8]

We will provide a detailed characterization of full-blooded exceptionalism in Section 1.3. Before proceeding, though, we would like to clarify what we take to be the conceptual relationship between these two ways of characterizing AEL. Arguably, a conception of logic which sees logic in strict continuity with the natural sciences is ipso facto a conception of logic which rejects most (if not all)

---

[7] This view is championed by Ben Martin and Ole Hjortland in Martin and Hjortland (2022).

[8] This label is inspired from the way in which Da Costa and Arenhart call their anti-exceptionalist conception of logic – *full-blooded anti-exceptionalism about logic* (see Da Costa & Arenhart 2018).

of the features that full-blooded exceptionalism – the purest exemplar of a traditional conception of logic – attributes to logic. In this respect, characterizing AEL in terms of continuity with the sciences entails a characterization of logic that rejects most (or all) of the features that the tradition attaches to logic (in other words, AEL-as-continuity entails AEL-as-tradition-rejection). In this respect, accepting a traditional conception – that is, accepting something in the vicinity of what we call "full-blooded exceptionalism" – means ipso facto to reject the idea that there is a significant continuity between logic and the sciences. Things are not so straightforward in relation to the converse entailment relation. Arguably there are ways of being anti-traditionalist about logic which do not necessarily see logic in strict continuity with the sciences. If that's correct, the characterization of AEL in terms of tradition-rejection does not by itself commit us to establish a continuity between logic and the sciences. In this respect, having both characterizations of AEL on board allows us to see that a commitment to an anti-exceptionalist thesis about logic comes somehow in degrees. For instance, an endorsement of a strict continuity between logic and the sciences matches what may be called a radical form of anti-exceptionalism (borrowing the label from Da Costa & Arenhart (2018) we may call it "full-blooded anti-exceptionalism"). However, there may be progressively milder forms of AEL based on a rejection of some of the traditional features of logic. Be that as it may, regardless of whether we take AEL as continuity or as tradition rejection, insofar as the former entails the latter and thus an acceptance of the traditional view of logic as exemplified by full-blooded exceptionalism entails a full rejection of the continuity thesis, it is helpful to dig deeper on what exactly are these characteristics traditionally associated with logic which AEL rejects. We do that by providing a characterization of full-blooded exceptionalism, to which we now turn.

1.3 On *Full-Blooded Exceptionalism*

Full-blooded exceptionalism is a view that takes logic to be fully general, formal, normative, analytic, necessary, a priori, and non-revisable.[9] We do not claim that full-blooded exceptionalism as such is a view that has been actually endorsed in the history of logic. We do, however, take it as a placeholder for a position that collects all the features that have been historically attributed to logic by a variety of philosophers and logicians.

---

[9] On the absolute (rational) unrevisability of logic see Hofweber (2021). See also Leech (2015) and Field (1996).

In this respect, its role in this Element is that of providing a neat paradigm of a view that exemplifies the various features that recent anti-exceptioanlist views have rejected (if not all, at least most of them). Let us analyze the features of full-blooded exceptionalism in some detail.

We begin with **Generality**, a feature that has been almost universally associated with logic.[10] An easy way to understand the *generality* of logic is to argue that, unlike the laws of biology, chemistry and physics, logical laws are typically conceived as wholly general, applying to all entities with no restrictions. In this regard, logical laws are considered to have the broadest scope of all laws, applying universally to everything without exception. On a minimalist interpretation, the generality of logical laws could be seen as exceptional only in a quantitative sense – having a higher, perhaps the highest, degree of generality – rather than in a qualitative sense – that is, as marking a substantive difference in nature between logic and the natural sciences. This conception of generality is best understood when combined with the, perhaps controversial, idea that quantification in logical truths (such as "for every x, either x is F or x is not F") is taken to be absolutely unrestricted. – that is, as requiring the existence of an all-inclusive domain of quantification.[11]

Historically, however, the notion of generality has been tied to various ideas traditionally associated with logic, giving it a less minimalist interpretation and aligning it more with a substantive sense of exceptionalism concerning the nature of logic. These ideas include, among others, the Kantian perspective that logical laws are universal and necessary and constitutive of rationality; Frege's thought that his logical system (the *Begriffsschrift*) is like the language Leibniz sketched, a *lingua characteristica*; Wittgenstein's notion of logical truths in the *Tractatus*, which posits that logical truths lack proper meaning as they do not limit the realm of possibilities; and finally, Carnap's belief in logical truths as analytic truths.

In the Kantian perspective, logic is a general art of reason (*canonical Epicuri*) dealing exclusively with *general*, namely universal and necessary, laws of thought. Logic is based on a priori principles, from which it is possible to derive all its rules, understood as rules to which all knowledge should conform. Such principles are independent of any content and are therefore determinable a priori.

Frege too viewed logic as a fully general discipline. As van Heijenoort points out (van Heijenoort 1967), Frege's belief in the superiority of his *Begriffsschrift*

---

[10] Contemporary exceptions to the generality of logic are Da Costa & Arenhart (2018) and Payette & Wyatt (2018).

[11] See the collection of papers edited by Agustin Rayo (Rayo 2009) for a discussion about absolute generality.

over Boole's algebraic logic was rooted precisely in the higher degree of generality of his system which was taken to provide a universal language for science.

Within the perspective of the early Wittgenstein's conception of logic, the *generality* feature is conceived as an essential trait of logic. In the *Tractatus* the idea that logical propositions are tautologies which say nothing and thus do not deal with any subject matter is coupled with the idea that they represent the scaffolding of the world (Wittgenstein 1921: 6.124). From such a point of view, it is clear that logic is quite distinct from the natural sciences (as well as from psychology or any social science) and not because it had a subject matter that could not be investigated by these sciences, but rather because logic *did not have* a subject matter at all. In line with the broader neo-positivist conception of logic which conceived of logical laws as lacking inherent meaning, Wittgenstein took the propositions of logic to be tools to demonstrate how language functions. According to this conception, the primary purpose of logical propositions is to illustrate how language operates as well as to reveal the relationships occurring among linguistic expressions of various kinds. This is achieved by means of an appropriate formalization of a sentence or an argument of natural language in a logical language: and the idea is that this process uncovers aspects of the nature and structure of natural language, aspects that might otherwise remain concealed by the grammatical surface of natural language expressions. Carnap, building upon this foundation, emphasizes that the validation and legitimacy of logical propositions are rooted in the rules that govern language. These rules include the formation of expressions and the procedures for inference and transformation.

Generality is thus the first element which is characteristic of full-blooded exceptionalism about logic – an element, as we will see, that is generally kept also in various anti-exceptionalist conceptions.

The second feature of exceptionality that we would like to discuss is the **Formality** feature. The notion of generality of logic has been linked, for example, by Kant and, more recently by Gila Sher, to a second crucial characteristic of full-blooded exceptionalism, namely that of the *formality* of logic, which is often understood in terms of *topic-neutrality*.[12] In his PhD thesis

---

[12] The concept of *topic neutrality* was introduced by Gilbert Ryle who used the following criterion for detecting topic-neutrality: "We may call English expressions 'topic-neutral' if a foreigner who understood them, but only them, could get no clue at all from an English paragraph containing them what that paragraph was about" – Ryle (1954: 116). Haack (1978) and Wright (1983) connect topic-neutrality with "formality," as does Ryle.

John MacFarlane distinguishes three senses of formality.[13] He says that logic is formal:

(1) in the sense that it provides constitutive norms for thought as such,
(2) in the sense that it is indifferent to the particular identities of objects, and
(3) in the sense that it abstracts entirely from the semantic content of thought. (MacFarlane 2000: ii)

Although the first sense of formality is not very prominent in contemporary debates,[14] it played a central role in Kant's philosophy. In fact, Kant is typically considered the founder of the tradition of seeing logic as formal. As MacFarlane points out,[15] in Kant's framework of transcendental idealism the first sense of formality illustrates more properly the generality of logic, rather than its formality, and is taken to entail the third sense of formality – which is Kant's favorite way of interpreting in what sense logic is said to be formal.

Besides Kant's own view on the issue, and moving to a more contemporary perspective, the second and the third senses of formality are those that have received more attention in recent literature. These two senses of formality have been clearly and directly linked to the notion of topic-neutrality: while the second sense offers an understanding of topic-neutrality in ontological terms where logic's characteristic notions and laws are taken to be indifferent to the particular identities of objects (they are all the same, logicwise), the third sense takes topic-neutrality as a semantic notion, where logic is said to abstract completely from the semantic contents of statements and inferences. As MacFarlane argues, while these three senses of formality may line up neatly in certain philosophical frameworks in others they can come apart.[16] Consequently, the first sense of formality does not imply either the second or third sense. In this regard, these three senses of formality are at least partially independent.[17]

As mentioned at the beginning of this section, it is customary to connect generality and formality via the concept of topic-neutrality – to the point that these three notions become highly connected and difficult to disentangle. Gila Sher has recently emphasized the intimate link between generality, formality, and topic-neutrality:

> Logic, on the present conception, takes certain general laws of formal structure and, using the machinery of logical terms, turns them into general laws of

---

[13] MacFarlane (2000).
[14] For a contemporary defense of a constitutivist view of logic along the lines of Kant's approach, refer to Leech (2015).
[15] See MacFarlane (2000) chapter 4.
[16] See MacFarlane (2000) chapters 4 and 5 for a thorough discussion of some views on formality, especially Kant's and Frege's views.
[17] MacFarlane argues for a full claim of independence of these three senses of formality, showing that neither the second sense nor the third sense of formality entails the first and, moreover, that the second and third sense of formality can come apart – see MacFarlane (2000): 66–68.

reasoning, applicable in any field of discourse. The fact that biological, physical, psychological, historical, [...] structures obey the general laws of formal structure explains the generality ("topic neutrality") of logic: some references to formal structure (to complements and unions of properties, identity of individuals, non-emptiness of extensions, etc.) is interwoven in all discourse, and therefore logic (the logic of negation and disjunction, identity, existential quantification, etc.) is universally applicable. (Sher 1996: 674–675)

Besides its link to the notion of generality, the formality of logic understood as topic-neutrality has a long tradition which counts many prominent logicians such as De Morgan, Frege, Russell, and Tarski. They write:

"Logic inquires into the form of thought, as separable from and independent of the matter thought of." (De Morgan 1858, reprinted in De Morgan 1966 – citation is from De Morgan 1966: 75)

"What is of concern to logic is not the special content of any particular relation, but only the logical form." (Frege 1953 [1884]: §70)

"Thus the absence of all mention of particular things or properties in logic or pure mathematics is a necessary result of the fact that this study is, as we say, 'purely formal'." (Russell 1920: 198)

Since we are concerned here with the concept of logical, i.e., formal, consequence, and thus with a relation which is to be uniquely determined by the form of the sentences between which it holds, this relation cannot be influenced in any way by empirical knowledge, and in particular by knowledge of the objects to which the sentence X or the sentences of the class K refer. The consequence relation cannot be affected by replacing the designations of the objects referred to in these sentences by the designations of any other objects. (Tarski 1936: 414–415)

These are just a few passages that illustrate the centrality of the notion of formality in logic. Its importance is strengthened by the fact that formality, especially in the second sense specified by MacFarlane, has been indicated as the chief criterion for demarcating logic by many logicians with quite different philosophical views on the nature of logic. In particular, formality in the second sense has been formalized as a criterion of logicality in terms of the notion of *permutation invariance* (now understood in terms of *isomorphism invariance*)[18]: logical terms are not altered by arbitrary permutations of the domain of discourse.[19]

---

[18] Some of the originators (but not Lindstrom) of the debate used the notion of permutation invariance, and some people continue with this today. However, as Gila Sher and Van McGee has pointed out, the notion of permutation invariance faces insurmountable problems with permutation (see Sher 1991; McGee 1996). Today, no one question that permutation is incorrect. We will discuss the notion of isomorphism invariance later on (see Section 4).

[19] For some very recent work on invariance criteria, see Bonnay & Speitel (2021), Paseau & Griffiths (2022), and Sagi (2022, 2024).

Let us now introduce a third feature which is at the core of exceptionalist conceptions of logic, namely the *Aprioricity* feature of logic. In delving into *full-blooded exceptionalism*, a fundamental philosophical quandary centers on the nature of our epistemic access to logical laws – in particular on whether our justification and/or knowledge of logical laws can be fundamentally obtained by a priori means,[20] as exceptionalists would claim. We take that the real epistemological hallmark of full-blooded exceptionalism is the thesis that knowledge and justification of logical principles are immune to any kind of empirical defeater (be it an underminer or an overrider). This does not mean that a full-blooded exceptionalist excludes the possibility of any kind of revision. Full-blooded exceptionalists should allow for the possibility of revising logical principles – unless they adopt a strong constitutivist thesis (as in Leech 2015) according to which certain basic logical principles cannot be rationally doubted because they are normatively constitutive of thought. However, such revisions would have to occur through a priori means, for example, by considerations pertaining to semantic paradoxes interpreted as providing a priori defeaters of a certain principles of classical logic. As we will see in the following sections, the question whether logic is open, at least in principle, to revision on the basis of empirical evidence is a recurrent and crucial theme in the exceptionalism/anti-exceptionalism debate – at least since the influential works of Hilary Putnam on quantum logic.[21]

A fourth crucial respect in which logic is taken to be exceptional has to do with the *analytic* character of its principles. Many historical figures such as Kant, Frege, Carnap, and other logical empiricists,[22] took logical statements to be analytic – that is, true in virtue of meaning (or the conventions of language) alone. As Ayer puts it, "the criterion of an analytic proposition is that its validity should follow simply from the definition of the terms contained in it" (Ayer 1936: 82).

For Carnap, and more generally for logical empiricists, the analyticity of logic served a double purpose. On the one hand, it helped to keep a broadly naturalistic outlook of our scientific knowledge where logic (and mathematics) can find their place into a natural scientific whole. On the other hand, it was instrumental to account for the idea that logical principles are necessary without having to rely on a spooky conception of metaphysical necessity.

---

[20] For a recent critical introduction to the topic of the a priori see Warren (2022).

[21] See, in particular Putnam (1968). Putnam's proposal have been challenged by many philosophers, including, notably, Dummett (Dummett 1976) and Kripke (Kripke 2023). Putnam himself officially retracted the view later on, on different grounds, as made explicit in Putnam (2005).

[22] For a recent introduction to Logical Empiricism see Richardson (2023).

Related to these points, the methods of logic offer a precise and comprehensive tool to clarify the negative claims about metaphysics. Logic demonstrates that the supposed claims of metaphysics involve concepts that cannot be defined through empirical means. Therefore, it precisely explains the grounds for dismissing such claims: not because they are untrue or subjective, but because they are, strictly speaking, devoid of meaning.[23] Interestingly, however, assessing metaphysics as meaningless based on linguistic grounds raises questions about the status of logical (and mathematical) claims, which also do not concern empirical reality and are meant to get their truth in a uniquely non-empirical way. As Quine claims:

> What now of the empiricist who would grant certainty to logic, and to the whole of the mathematics, and yet would make a clean sweep of other non-empirical theories under the name of metaphysics? The Viennese solution to this nice problem was predicated on language. Metaphysics was meaningless through misuse of language; logic was certain through tautologous use of language. (Quine 1963: 386)

Quine notoriously rejected what he called "the linguistic doctrine of logical truth" and the underlying distinction between analytic and synthetic statements. As a consequence of Quine's famous attacks on the notion of analyticity (see Quine 1951) and on the notion of truth by convention (Quine 1936, 1963), the philosophical community has mostly accepted the fact that no sound notion of metaphysical analyticity could be concocted.[24] For instance, Boghossian agrees with Quine that the traditional conception of analyticity is fundamentally flawed. However, in a series of influential papers (Boghossian 1996; Boghossian & Williamson 2020), he develops an epistemic notion of analyticity. He argues that this new conception of analyticity stands independently from the traditional (metaphysical) notion of analyticity and is not vulnerable to Quine's wide-ranging criticisms. According to Boghossian, a sentence is "epistemically analytic if grasp of its meaning can suffice for justified belief in the truth of the proposition it expresses" (Boghossian 2003: 15). When applied to logic, the idea is that being willing to infer according to modus ponens is meaning-constitutive of the ordinary concept "if, then," and this fact explains our being entitled to reason in accordance with modus ponens, even if the inference is, as Boghossian puts it "blind – unsupported by any positive

---

[23] This is a consequence of their verificationist theory of meaning, the core idea of which was that only claims with clear (empirical) verification conditions, that is, claims framed in a language of pure experience (or any logical composition of such claims), were meaningful.

[24] But see Warren (2020) for a rejoinder.

warrant" (Boghossian 2003: 23).[25] Boghossian's concept of epistemic analyticity has faced various criticisms, with some of the most influential coming from Williamson in a series of papers, collected in Boghossian and Williamson (2020).

Finally, the last feature of *full-blooded exceptionalism* that we would like to discuss is **Normativity**. An exceptionalist conception of the normativity of logic, which would fit well with full-blooded exceptionalism, takes logic to be a normative discipline. As Frege claimed: "Like ethics, logic can also be called a normative science" (Frege 1979: 128). Setting aside interpretive questions about what Frege truly believed regarding the normativity of logic (a complex issue, as Frege appears to endorse seemingly contradictory claims),[26] one could argue for the strong thesis that logic, like ethics, is a normative discipline, and its laws, much like ethical laws, should be understood in normative-deontic terms. One way to cast this view out is to take full-blooded exceptionalists to be committed to the view that logical principles (unlike principles or laws of any other science, e.g., physics) are intrinsically *normative* for reasoning. More precisely, in this view logical principles are taken to be the source of a kind of normativity which provides reasoners with *normative guidance* as to what to believe or disbelieve in the context of reasoning. Roughly, the idea is that logic, by its very nature, engenders some constraints (the precise character and scope of which are a matter of debate) on what doxastic attitude to have in relation to premises and conclusion of a logically valid argument. To give an example, one may think that logic, or, better, its core notion of validity, exerts something like the following constraint: that a subject ought not to disbelieve a conclusion C which, as a matter of logic, follows from a set of premises P1, ... Pn, under the condition that she believes all the premises.[27] Moreover – the exceptionalist about logical normativity typically maintains – such constraints are entirely sourced in the nature of logic (and logical principles) and not in some extrinsic factors, like truth, rationality, or knowledge.

---

[25] This strategy should be adjusted in order to avoid gaining entitlement to certain inferences concerning epistemically defective concepts such as "tonk," "boche," and "flurg." This requires some restrictions on the meaning-entitlement connection that we are not able to discuss properly in the limited space of this Element: Very roughly, the idea is to take some meaningful term in a language as "expressing a concept that conditionalizes on the existence of an appropriate semantic value for it" (Boghossian 2003: 23).

[26] See Mezzadri (2015a, 2015b) for a thorough discussion of Frege's conception of the normativity of logic.

[27] This is an example of what MacFarlane has labeled a *bridge principle* (i.e., principles that bridge logical facts about validity with normative constraints concerning which combinations of doxastic attitudes to have toward the relata of the validity relation). This particular instance is what MacFarlane taxonomizes as a deontic principle with wide scope and negative polarity (WO-: you ought to see to it that if you believe A and you believe B, you do not disbelieve C). See MacFarlane (2004).

Historically, Kant, Frege, and Carnap in different ways argued that logic's normative constraints extend beyond limiting just reasoning and encompass all forms of thinking. This is usually specified by claiming that logical laws are normatively constitutive of thinking. Normative constitutivism is the thesis that no kind of cognitive practice whose correctness conditions allow for breaches of logical laws can count as thinking. While this does not exclude forms of illogical thinking as instances of thinking, it excludes that any kind of illogical thinking is *correct* thinking: in other words, no correct thinking can be illogical. Normative constitutivism is one way in which an exceptionalist conception of the normativity of logic can be developed.[28]

Alternatively, one may subscribe to a more moderate understanding of logic's normative role as extrinsic and instrumental on the achievement of truth. In this second, more moderate understanding of logic's normativity, logic would retain a normative role with respect to thinking and reasoning but without being a normative discipline (and in this sense it would be different from ethics, and more akin to the sciences). As MacFarlane observes, even if logical laws are not prescriptive in their content, they imply prescriptions about asserting, thinking, judging, inferring.[29] What would be distinctive of the logical laws, even in this picture, is their scope: they "prescribe universally the way in which one ought to think if one is to think at all" (Frege 1893: xv). In this sense they should be considered more general than laws of the sciences like for example physics. Indeed, unlike the laws governing sciences such as geometry or physics, the laws of logic transcend specific objects or properties associated with any particular discipline. They operate on a more fundamental level, independent of specific entities or attributes that might be explored within a particular field of study (see Ricketts 1985: 4–5). One way to cast this out is to follow the Fregean tradition and conceive of rules of inference as principles endowed with *normative force*, where their normative force derives from the meaning of the logical constants. In this picture an expression's meaning is equated with its role in determining the circumstances under which a statement containing that expression would be deemed true. As for logical constants, the meaning is represented, in the simplest and most typical case, by the way the truth value of the entire sentence depends on the truth values of the components, and the formulation of the logical rules assumes that their meaning is already fixed. In this context,

---

[28] Contemporary versions of logical constitutivism are proposed by Jessica Leech (Leech 2015), who endorses an intrinsicist form of normative constitutivism about logical normativity, and by Manish Oza (Oza 2020), who develops what he takes to be an extrinsicist variant of the constitutivist thesis. For a different strategy in favor of an intrinsicist thesis see Ferrari & Hlobil (forthcoming).

[29] See MacFarlane (2002).

rules of inference are deemed normative not because they dictate a specific course of epistemic action, as it were, but rather because they elucidate something imbued with normative features: the disposition to make inferences based on meaning.[30]

1.4 Full-Blooded Exceptionalism and Natural Sciences. A First Comparison

Now, even conceding that, as Rossberg and Shapiro observe, "[E]very form of inquiry, scientific or otherwise, is different, in crucial ways, from every other" (Rossberg & Shapiro 2021: 6430) it is certainly hard to deny that such a full-blooded exceptionalist conception of logic is in sharp contrast with the most reasonable conception of physics and other natural sciences – indeed, with any reasonable conception of the recognized sciences (perhaps, with the exception of mathematics, which may be taken, not so unreasonably, to enjoy a similar degree of exceptionality as logic does).

To illustrate in more detail, let's focus on physics. First, considering generality, physics certainly has a high degree of generality, but its subject matter is nevertheless restricted to physical matter (perhaps even to anything which has physical existence). Frege, for example, observes that physics concerns itself with laws governing phenomena like weight and heat (Frege 1918). Thus, the generality achieved by physics and fundamental physical laws falls short of the kind of absolute generality that, according to full-blooded exceptionalism, logical laws enjoy.

Second, physics, as the other recognized sciences, is not purely formal. Whether a certain law is a law of physics clearly depends on the nature of the objects and properties it is about. In this respect, the degree of invariance under permutation that physical laws enjoy is lower than that enjoyed by the laws of logic. Consider the laws of special relativity. These laws are invariant under permutations of inertial reference-frames. They remain invariant in all such frames. In other words, they are not affected by replacements of one inertial frame by another.[31] However, they are not invariant under a larger class of permutations.[32] Laws of physics (e.g., laws of thermodynamics) apply to all physical entities, but not to all kinds of entities – for example, they do not apply to numbers.

Third, physics deals with synthetic truths and our epistemic access to such truths is distinctively a posteriori since it heavily and essentially relies on

---

[30] This is, of course, just one possibility. Other sources of the normativity at issue could be truth, knowledge, or rationality.

[31] See Sher (2022: 31) for a discussion of this example.

[32] We will deal with permutation invariance as a criterion of logicality in Section 3.

empirical evidence and observation, *latu sensu*. In particular, physical theories are taken to be revisable on the basis of empirical evidence: a principle that is taken to be a law, but it is discovered by empirical observation not to be a law of physics should be abandoned.

Fourth, physics is taken to be descriptive: its primary, if not sole, task is to provide an accurate description of the physical reality. In this respect our best physical theory has normative consequences in the sense that believing things that are contrary to it is incorrect. However, this is taken to have nothing to do with the fact that it is physics we are talking about (or that the laws in question are *physical law*) but rather with the general normative principle that having false beliefs (about anything) is incorrect (under the plausible assumption that truth and falsity exert normative constraints on belief).[33]

Let us wrap up this section by highlighting, once more, that full-blooded exceptionalism is a rather peculiar position in the philosophy of logic. Furthermore, the accuracy of this description as a historically held position remains controversial. It may well be that historical figures such as Aristotle, Kant, Frege, the early Wittgenstein, perhaps more controversially Carnap, and more contemporary figures such as Michael Dummett, Hartry Field, Bob Hale, Saul Kripke, Jessica Leech, Gil Sagi, and Crispin Wright, among others, have adopted, to a variable degree, a somewhat exceptionalist conception of logic without subscribing to a full-blooded version of it. Be that as it may, as mentioned earlier, our primary objective in briefly introducing this radical, full-blooded, exceptionalist perspective on logic is dialectical. It serves to enhance our understanding of various anti-exceptionalist views in logic. In fact, given the number of aspects involved in the characterization of an exceptionalist stance toward logic, it seems clear that one may adopt an exceptionalist stance to a higher or lower degree, as it were. As a consequence of this flexibility in characterizing logical exceptionalism, it is hard to individuate a sharp boundary between what counts as an exceptionalist conception of logic and what counts, instead, as an anti-exceptionalist conception.

Section 2 will delve into the most radical objections to the core features of an exceptionalist conception of logic which we have outlined in this section. We will directly engage with the primary source of these objections, focusing on Quine and his philosophy of logic.

---

[33] There's a considerable debate on the question concerning whether, how and to what extent truth (and falsity) put normative constraints on inquiry. For a comprehensive discussion of the normative role of truth in inquiry, particularly in relation to disagreement, see Ferrari (2022) and the references cited therein.

2 Quine's Philosophy of Logic

2.1 Quine as the Precursor of Logical Anti-Exceptionalism

During the twentieth century, most of the core features of the full-blooded exceptionalist conception of logic illustrated in Section 1.3 have been radically criticized by a variety of leading philosophers such as Bertrand Russell, Willard Van Orman Quine, Hilary Putnam, Penelope Maddy, Gila Sher, Timothy Williamson, Gillian Russell, and still others. However, among these figures, nobody more than Quine contributed to the establishment of an anti-exceptionalist conception of logic as one of the most prevalent perspectives in contemporary debates within the philosophy of logic. As Ben Martin and Ole Hjortland write: "It is only with the advance of philosophical naturalism and Quine's writings that anti-exceptionalism received serious consideration in the philosophy of logic" (Martin & Hjortland 2024).

An interesting feature of Quine's conception of logic in the light of current debates within the philosophy of logic, in particular in relation to logical anti-exceptionalism, is that it merges the two senses of anti-exceptionalism introduced in Section 1.2. On the one hand, Quine emphasizes the similarity between logic and the sciences, arguing that their differences in epistemology and methodology are more about degree than substance. On the other hand, as a likely result of this view, Quine separates logic from certain traditional characteristics associated with it, particularly its being analytic and a priori. In this sense, and perhaps unsurprisingly, Quine's original stance toward logic brings together elements of LAE-as-continuity and elements of LAE-as-tradition-rejection. But let's proceed with a closer discussion of Quine's conception of logic in the broader context of Quine's philosophy. A word of caution: although Quine consistently adhered to a broadly anti-exceptionalist view of logic, his philosophical positions evolved over the course of his career. Some of the more radical theses from his early period were softened in his later, more mature, work. For the sake of brevity and clarity, we will set aside a historically and exegetically precise account of Quine's conception of logic. Instead, we will focus on the aspects of his views on logic that are most relevant to our discussion.

2.2 Quine's Reaction against the Logical Empiricist Conception of Logic

As John Burgess points out, "[V]irtually all Quine's philosophical writings, early and late, pertain directly or indirectly to logic, mathematics, or both" (Burgess 2014: 279). This is to say that Quine's views on the nature of logic (and mathematics) were pivotal in developing his philosophy. These views stemmed from a reaction against logical positivism, which was the prominent form of empiricism at the time when Quine began his career in philosophy. At the core of logical positivism there was a neat distinction between synthetic statements – namely, those statements that are open to empirical (dis)confirmation – and analytic statements – typically the statements of logic and mathematics that are true in virtue of meaning alone and thus fully immune to empirical (dis) confirmation. Logical positivists thus conceived of logic (and mathematics) as sharply distinct from the sciences from a broadly epistemological point of view. A clear statement of the logical positivist view on logic is given by Rudolph Carnap. Commenting on the approach of the Vienna Circle to the philosophy of logic and mathematics, Carnap writes:

> In this distinction we had seen the way out of the difficulty which had prevented the older empiricism from giving a satisfactory account of the nature of knowledge in logic and mathematics. [...] Our solution, based on Wittgenstein's conception, consisted in asserting the thesis of empiricism only for factual truth. By contrast, the truths in logic and mathematics are not in need of confirmation by observations, because they do not state anything about the world of facts, they hold for any possible combination of facts. (Carnap in Schilpp 1963: 64)

Thus, while scientific statements and theories deal with empirical (broadly observational) matters, logic (and logical theories) do not deal with empirical matters at all, their role being, roughly, that of tools needed to clarify the structure of our scientific knowledge of the world and systematize it.

Quine's opposition to the form of empiricism adopted by logical positivists led him to explicitly reject a number of core features of what we have called full-blooded exceptionalism about logic – features such as aprioricity, analyticity, necessity, and normativity. Even more broadly, Quine shattered some of the most resilient traditions and distinctions in philosophy. He rejected both rationalism and foundationalism by subscribing to a kind of philosophical naturalism coupled with a holistic model of knowledge. While his commitment to naturalism requires that all kinds of enquiries take empirical evidence to be the ultimate arbiter of a theory, his commitment to holism rejects the idea that single hypotheses are directly confirmed or disconfirmed by experience. Instead, it is the entire theory that faces the "tribunal of experience" collectively.

These commitments to naturalism and holism led Quine to argue that some distinctions which were deeply entrenched with the philosophical tradition – distinctions such as those between a priori/a posteriori knowledge, between analytic and synthetic truths, and between necessity and contingency – all collapse. In particular, the rejection of the distinction between analytic and synthetic statements is especially impactful in relation to the philosophy of logic.[34] As Quine writes:

> For, given the second dogma, analyticity is needed to account for the meaningfulness of logical and mathematical truths, which are clearly devoid of empirical content. But when we drop the second dogma and see logic and mathematics rather as meshing with physics and other sciences for the joint implication of empirical consequences, the question of limiting empirical content to some sentences at the expense of others no longer arises. (Quine 1986a: 207)

If logical statements are not devoid of empirical content they are exposed to the possibility of empirical confirmation as well as to the possibility of empirical disconfirmation.[35] Regarding empirical confirmation, as Crispin Wright puts it, the Quinean idea is "that the epistemic good standing of logical principles is properly earned in the same way as the confirmation of all empirical-scientific laws. We are justified in accepting such principles by, and only by, their participation in ongoing successful scientific theory" (Wright 2021: 334). In this sense, the justification of logic, as well as the justification of any other scientific theory, is inferential and inseparable from the justification of the rest of our web of knowledge. And, perhaps even more controversially, Quine explicitly adhered to the thesis that no logical principle is immune to the possibility of revision. In an often cited passage from "Two Dogmas," Quine writes: "No statement is immune to revision. Revision even of the logical law of the excluded middle has been proposed as a means of simplifying quantum mechanics; and what difference is there in principle between such a shift and the shift whereby Kepler superseded Ptolemy, or Einstein Newton, or Darwin Aristotle?" (Quine 1951: 40).[36]

This is one of Quine's most direct statements of the idea that in line with any kind of scientific hypotheses, and all the rest of our knowledge, logical laws are in principle open to revision (on the basis of experience). A couple of pages later, Quine returns to the issue of the revisability of logic, contextualizing it within his holistic picture of meaning and confirmation:

> [T]otal science is like a field of force whose boundary conditions are experience. A conflict with experience at the periphery occasions readjustments in the interior of the field. Truth-values have to be redistributed over some of our

---

[34] See Burge (2003) for a detailed critical assessment of Quine's arguments.

[35] Although these two principles are part-and-parcel of Quine's picture of what it is to rationally manage a system of empirical beliefs, they are separable claims, as Wright points out, and can be dealt with independently of each other (see Wright 2021 for a criticism of both principles).

[36] More properly, it's revision of one of the classically valid distributivity principles that was proposed.

statements. Re-evaluation of some statements entails re-evaluation of others, because of their logical interconnections – *the logical laws being in turn simply certain further statements of the system, certain further elements of the field*. Having re-evaluated one statement we must re-evaluate some others, which may be statements logically connected with the first or may be the statements of logical connections themselves. (Quine 1951: 42, our emphasis)

This amounts to a straight rejection of one of the most central epistemological tenets of full-blooded exceptionalism. If our best logical theory, let's say a system of classical logic explicitly schematized in propositional form, runs into some recalcitrant experience when used in our scientific endeavors, say, because of the discovery of certain quantum phenomena, then adjusting one of its principles, say, one of the distributivity principle, is perfectly fine if such an adjustment is in fact the most effective way of ironing out the wrinkles. This is in line with, in fact an instance of, Quine's holistic approach according to which whenever our scientific practice encounters a situation of recalcitrance, it is in principle rational to hold responsible not just the empirical scientific premises, but any aspects of our knowledge of the world, including the underlying logic involved in deriving the consequence of the specific scientific practice under scrutiny. Clearly, Quine's form of logical anti-exceptionalism, particularly as presented in his 1951 work, retains a significant element of empiricism, albeit "without the dogmas." In essence, Quine still views sensory experience as the boundary condition for science. But, as Williamson aptly notes, "that experience has any such unique privilege is not a truism, unless 'experience' is just another word for learning" (Williamson 2024: 416).

However, despite the fact that in Quine's holistic picture nothing is in principle immune to revision, it is still the case that in the practice of reassessing our knowledge on the basis of recalcitrant evidence, logic and mathematics enjoy some privileged status. As a matter of fact, Quine takes the vulnerability to revision to be a matter of degree: "It is at a minimum in logic and mathematics, because disruptions here would reverberate so widely through science. [. . .] Basic laws of physics, such as those of physical geometry or of conservation, are a little more vulnerable. There is a grading off. Toward the observational periphery of the fabric of science, vulnerability increases" (Quine 1986b: 620).

This is known in the literature as the maxim of minimal mutilation, and it consists in the thought that when revising belief systems or theoretical systems to accommodate new information, recalcitrant data, or solve inconsistencies, one should make the least number of changes necessary to resolve the issues, thus *mutilating* the original belief system as little as possible. In Quine's own words: "If revisions are seldom proposed that cut so deep as to touch logic, there is a clear enough reason for that: the maxim of minimum mutilation. The maxim suffices to explain the air of necessity that attaches to logical and mathematical truth" (Quine 1986a: 100).

Thus, according to Quine, our reluctance to revise logical principles in the face of recalcitrant evidence, even in those situations where revising logic may not sound too far-fetched as – someone may claim – in the case of quantum phenomena, is due to the privileged position that logic occupies in the web of belief – namely, right at the center of it. Given this centrality of logic in the web of belief, a request for revision of our logical theory should be the very last resort, when no other adjustments in the web seem to tame the recalcitrant observations. Because of its core position and role within our total theory of the world, revising logic would be extremely costly (a change in logic would require a change in almost anything else). That's why Quine didn't think that the various phenomena (linguistic, such as vagueness or other logico-semantic paradoxes, and non-linguistic, such as quantum phenomena) that some have taken to put pressure on some principles of classical logic were regarded by Quine as not sufficiently strong to require a revision of classical logic.

Additionally, as the quote earlier makes clear, the maxim of minimal mutilation also explains the *air of necessity* that surrounds the truths of logic. Clearly, the very expression that Quine uses – namely, "air of necessity" – vividly suggests that for Quine there's no distinct kind of logical necessity that attaches to logical truths. Rather, as Haack points out (Haack 1975: 238) the practical immunity to revision of classical logic is the closest Quine gets to the thesis that the laws of classical logic are necessary. This is a notion of necessity which falls considerably short of the strong sense of necessity attached to logical laws by advocates of full-blooded exceptionalism. After all, it could happen that in response to recalcitrant experience, we opt for revising our logic rather than revising something else, like physics. And there's no reason to exclude that in principle someday experience will lead us to revise our logic.

Thus, we have seen that Quine rejected some of the core ideas of logical exceptionalism namely: that logical statements are analytic; that they cannot be justified or revised on the basis of empirical evidence; and that they enjoy a distinctive kind of necessity. We should now add that, as a consequence of his general naturalistic and holistic approach to philosophy and, more specifically, the epistemology of logic, Quine rejects the idea that logic is normative in any interesting sense. There's no set of prescriptions or proscriptions (how we ought or ought not to reason) that are distinctively logical – namely, proscriptions or prescriptions that are not derived from or grounded in, for instance, the norms provided by truth and falsity. This does not mean that Quine's epistemology is completely free of any normative considerations, but these considerations have only the rather minimal function of "warning us against telepaths and soothsayers" (Quine 1990: 19) – and thus against the employment of methods of investigation (and reasoning) that are unreliable (broadly non-truth-conducive). Insofar as logic deals with truths, logic has a normative role to play in preventing us from accumulating falsehoods in reasoning from true premises in accordance with logical principles. This is fully in accordance with anti-normativist theses, like the one of Gillian Russell (Russell 2020), according to which logic isn't normative in any interesting sense: its normative role is purely ancillary to the normative role of truth in inquiry.

2.3 Some Elements of Continuity with Logical Exceptionalism

Although Quine's conception of logic is in sharp contrast, both methodologically and epistemologically, with some of the core features of full-blooded exceptionalism, there are nevertheless some points on which Quine's view is in continuity with a traditional conception.

One of these features has to do with the generality of logic – a feature that, with Quine, the vast majority of contemporary anti-exceptionalists keep on board.[37] Being an anti-exceptionalist about the scope of logic would be to adhere to a kind of logical particularism, for which Quine did not express any sympathy. As Quine writes, "Trivially [...] the logical truths are true by virtue of any circumstances you care to name – language, the world, anything" (Quine 1986a: 96). Relatedly, logic (as well as mathematics) can be contrasted with the rest of science in terms of its "versatility: [its] vocabulary pervades all branches of science" (Quine 1986c: 402).

Let's dig deeper on this point of continuity between Quine's conception of logic and logical exceptionalism. First of all, observe that Quine claims that the best way to regiment a theory, for example a scientific theory, is using the syntax of classical first-order logic with identity. The reason is that he considers the syntax of classical first-order logic with identity to be clear, powerful, simple, and, especially, transparent – namely, what you see is what you get in terms of what is expressed by a sentence regimented in first-order logic. Secondly, Quine accepts that classical first-order logic is topic-neutral. As Quine expresses the point, logic "has no objects it can call its own; its variables admit all values indiscriminately" (Quine 1995: 52). Indeed, even if for Quine a priori arguments may not resolve in a definite manner ontological questions, these matters find their resolution through the selection of a canonical notation, which, in turn,

---

[37] The only notable exceptions we know of are provided by two papers: the first, by Payette and Wyatt's paper "Logical Particularism" (see Payette & Wyatt 2018); the second by Da Costa and Arenhart's paper "Full-Blooded Anti-Exceptionalism" (see Da Costa & Arenhart 2018) where they defend what they call a *localist* conception of logic.

is guided by the pursuit of overall systematic simplicity. Let us take a look at the two aforementioned elements of Quine's conception of logic.

As for the first reason, for Quine, the syntax of classical first-order logic with identity is a powerful tool for regimenting a theory. Using it, we clarify its ontological commitments. Indeed, we owe to Quine the formulation of the most well-known criterion for identifying a theory's T ontological commitments. The process involves the following steps:

1. We first translate the theory T into the canonical notation of a first-order logical language with identity.
2. We then consider the set of all statements that are formal consequences of the theory T – namely, the theorems of T.
3. Further, we select those members of this set that begin with (at least) one existential quantification (i.e., with an existential quantifier "∃" followed by a variable, let's call it "x"; the resulting expression "∃x" reads as "there is at least one object x") whose scope is the rest of the statement. These are the statements that reveal the ontological commitment of a theory T.
4. We then address the following question: what things must be in the domain as values of variables for the theorems of T that begin with an existential quantifier to be true?

According to Quine, the answer to this last question provides the ontological commitment of a theory T, exemplified with the Quinean well-known slogan: "To be is, purely and simply, to be the value of a bound variable" (Quine 1948: 32). For example, consider a theory T that has only the following statement in English as its axiom:

(S) Some dogs are black.

We can translate the statement (S) into the notation of first-order logic:

(S*) ∃x (x is a dog & x is black).

One of the consequences of our axiom will be the statement "∃x (x is a dog)" and this statement is a theorem of T that begins with the existential quantifier "∃." If we ask the question: "What things must fall in the domain as variable values in order for theorems of T that begin with a quantifier to be true?" one answer will be "dogs." Thus, we conclude that theory T will be ontologically committed to dogs. It should be noted that according to Quine regardless of what is exactly the domain of quantification, one always speaks of existence in the same sense, and there is nothing to prevent one from using the same notion of existence in relation to a mixed domain of dromedaries and numbers, or even an all-encompassing domain of all things.

Classical first-order logic with identity is the syntactic tool to qualify the ontological commitments of a theory. From this point of view, it does not depart from many classical conceptions of logic. His reasons to privilege classical first-order logic in evaluating the ontological commitment of a theory are that classical logic has a complete proof procedure and it is ontologically innocent (Hylton 2007: 265ff). Indeed, Quine seems committed to the view that only classical first-order logic is *logic proper* due to its completeness, while extensions of logic are classified as mathematics (Quine 1986a: 91). In particular, classical logic has a complete proof procedure for validity and for inconsistency. And either procedure suffices, since a formula is valid if and only if its negation is inconsistent. The completeness of first-order logic shows how to give a syntactic account of first-order logical implication, without presuppositions. Specifically, as Hylton argues, it is possible to define logical truth and validity without presupposing truth and interpretation (Hylton 2007: 266). As Quine himself points out, "[completeness] shows that we can define logical truth by mere description of a proof procedure, without loss of any traits that made logical truth interesting to us in the first place" (Quine 1986a: 57).[38]

Consider that in his perspective classical first-order logic permits multiple distinct yet equivalent approaches to logical truths. Within classical logic, one can define logical truth through model theory, substitution, or proof theory – and the latter method is specifically viable because classical logic admits a complete proof procedure. Quine's preference leans toward the substitutional definition rather than the model-theoretic one, primarily because the latter relies on set theory (Quine 1986a: 55).

Classical first-order logic is also considered by Quine ontologically innocent; and this brings us back to the second element of continuity between Quine's view on logic and the full-blooded exceptionalist perspective. The reason why Quine thinks that logic is ontologically innocent is not because it avoids commitments to any kind of entity; rather, it is because it avoids commitments to entities that are problematic – such as intensional entities which Quine in some of his earlier works famously labeled "creatures of darkness."[39]

What first-order logic does require is the acceptance of at least one object in existence, without imposing any presuppositions regarding the nature of this object. In this respect it is essential to establish a clear definition of entities that can be deemed as non-problematic. Classical first-order logic is viewed by Quine as ontologically unproblematic. Quine has two reasons for that. First,

---

[38] In his *Philosophy of Logic* (Quine 1986a), Quine contrasts classical first-order logic with second order logic which he considers "a wolf in sheep's clothing" – a piece of mathematics, disguised as logic. On this point, see Smid (2020).

[39] See Quine (1956: 180).

predicates (and other non naming expressions) do not require a corresponding entity to be meaningful. Thus, the admission of properties to make sense of truths is, in general, dispensable. Quine invites us to reflect on the fact that properties or propositions lack explanatory power and clear identity criteria. It is precisely for this reason that they are not admissible entities. Take, for example, the case of propositions. Quine's argument for their exclusion runs in the following way: No entity is admissible if we are not able to express the truth-conditions of statements of the form "*a* is identical with *b*" in a determinate way. Propositions are identical if the statements expressing them are synonymous. This is the only way to have an identity criterion for propositions. But, on the one hand, there is insufficient *behavioral* evidence for synonymy. On the other hand, *behavioral* evidence is the only evidence available for synonymy. If so, there is no identity criterion for propositions. As a consequence there are no propositions. Objects, on the contrary, exhibit the opposite virtues: they have explanatory power and clearer identity criteria. Secondly, Quine emphasizes that classical first-order logic "has no objects it can call its own; its variables admit all values indiscriminately" (Quine 1995: 52). This perspective suggests that classical logic's appeal lies in its neutrality toward the subject matter.

In sum, although Quine's views on logic do not amount to the most radical kind of anti-exceptionalism to date, it is indisputable that Quine played a crucial role in challenging some of the core characteristics of the traditional conception of logic. Moreover, Quine explicitly endorsed the view that there is a significant continuity, methodological and epistemological, between logic and the sciences – their differences being more a matter of degree than of substance. The recent and ongoing debates in the epistemology of logic demonstrate the profound and extensive influence of Quine's conception of logic.

3 Demarcation in Science

3.1 Demarcation Problems: Logic and Science

Our primary objective in this section and the subsequent two is to explore the demarcation issue in both logic and science, delving into the nuances and intricacies that characterize and differentiate these fields. Although we cannot reasonably hope to say anything innovative on the general issue of demarcation in the context of this Element, we believe that a systematic discussion of how to set the boundary between science and non-science, on the one hand, and between logic and non-logic, on the other hand, may help us put into sharper focus the main question at the core of this Element – namely the question of whether and to what extent logic is a science. Our hope is that this brief discussion will advance our understanding, particularly in the context of the anti-exceptionalism debate.

It seems fair to say that the debate on logical anti-exceptionalism has, until now, been characterized by limited and sometimes vague discussions about the supposed scientific status or the anti-exceptional nature of logic. In fact, in examining the current state of the debate, it is clear that many logicians and philosophers of logic readily suggest that logic closely resembles a science. However, they often hesitate to delve into discussions about what it precisely means for logic to be considered a science. Regardless of the current state of the debate in the philosophy of logic, we maintain that the question of whether, and to what extent, logic qualifies as a science is not only philosophically significant but also important and inherently complex. Consequently, it warrants a more focused and detailed discussion. That being said, it is important to clarify that the primary aim of discussing demarcation criteria in relation to logical anti-exceptionalism is not to argue that a sensible anti-exceptionalist stance on logic requires a strict set of criteria for distinguishing science from non-science. Rather, the goal is to show that a more nuanced understanding of these criteria and their interconnections offers a clearer picture of what it means to be an anti-exceptionalist about logic, and to what extent.

To begin with, we take it that when we inquire into whether and to what extent logic is a science, we end up engaging with three, undoubtedly intricate, issues at once, namely: (i) the issue of what counts as logic (i.e.: how do we demarcate logic from non-logic?); (ii) the issue of what counts as science (i.e.: how do we demarcate science from non-science?); (iii) the issue of whether logic meets (some or all of) the demarcation criteria for being a science (i.e.: does logic qualify as a science?). The plan for this section and the subsequent two is thus to discuss these three questions and to provide some useful indication concerning how to address them in relation to the aim of advancing the debate on anti-exceptionalism about logic. Let's start with the issue of how to demarcate science from non-science.

3.2 Demarcation Problems in Science

"Science"[40] is one of those terms that we, as competent users of a natural language living in a society heavily relying on technological and scientific knowledge, are all acquainted with. We inherently grasp an intuitive, though somewhat vague, distinction between what qualifies as science and what does

---

[40] Contrary to the usage by Boudry (2017: 38) and Hansson (2013: 63–65), who employ "science" as a broad equivalent to the German concept "Wissenschaft" encompassing all academic research fields, we will limit our use of "science" to primarily denote the natural sciences. This aligns with the conventional understanding of the term in British and American English.

not. Indeed, it is rare to find someone who would argue against physics being a science, while categorizing divination as one. However, the task of establishing a clear-cut criterion to distinguish what qualifies as science from what does not has proven to be extremely challenging. This challenge has led many philosophers to abandon the demarcation issue for an extended period, viewing it as unsolvable and therefore not worth pursuing. More recently, the research on demarcation made a timid comeback especially in relation to the spreading of science denialism and pseudoscientific disinformation. In this regard, we find ourselves in agreement with Imre Lakatos' assertion that "the demarcation between science and pseudoscience is not merely a problem of armchair philosophy: it is of vital social and political relevance" (Lakatos 1978: 1). In this section, our aim is to highlight the key elements of the discussion surrounding the demarcation problem throughout the twentieth century.

Before delving into this task, it is important to note from the outset that the type of demarcation quest prevalent in debates within the philosophy of science operates at a broader level of granularity compared to the kind of demarcation we will be addressing in Section 4 in relation to logic. While our task there will be to delineate what (deductive) logic is (and is about) in order to demarcate at least part (albeit an important part) of the discipline of logic from other disciplines, the task that is before us in this section is concerned with the more general issue of delineating the broad field of scientific disciplines – as opposed to both pseudo-scientific and non-scientific disciplines. The goal, in this respect, is not to establish criteria for distinguishing between disciplines like physics, biology, and chemistry (just to mention three paradigmatic examples of scientific disciplines), but rather to identify the criteria by which all three are recognized as sciences.

With this in hand, let's proceed with discussing the issue of demarcation in science. There has been an important debate during the twentieth century about the so-called "demarcation problem."[41] The project behind this discussion was the rather ambitious one of providing a set of individually necessary and jointly sufficient conditions for deciding whether a certain theory or practice is scientific or unscientific (which includes both non-scientific as well as pseudo-scientific theories and practices). Success in finding such a set of necessary and sufficient conditions would provide us with a sharp demarcation criterion capable of determining, for any given candidate discipline whether it counts as scientific or not.

---

[41] Part of this discussion about the demarcation problem in science follows the discussion in Hansson (2021).

This ambitious project was particularly prominent during the heyday of logical positivism and logical empiricism and found its clearest expression throughout the influential work of Karl Popper. Given their staunch opposition to (traditional, mostly German) metaphysics, logical positivists of the Vienna Circle were interested primarily in providing a criterion for distinguishing scientific (and thus meaningful) claims from metaphysical (and thus meaningless) claims. Within this project, logic as a tool for the logical analysis of language had a prominent role. As Carnap sharply puts it:

> In the domain of *metaphysics*, including all philosophy of value and normative theory, logical analysis yields the negative result *that the alleged statements in this domain are entirely meaningless*. Therewith a radical elimination of metaphysics is attained. [...] In saying that the so-called statements of metaphysics are *meaningless*, we intend this word in its strictest sense [according to which] a sequence of words is *meaningless* if it does not, within a specified language, constitute a statement. It may happen that such a sequence of words looks like a statement at first glance; in that case we call it a *pseudo-statement*: Our thesis, now, is that logical analysis reveals the alleged statements of metaphysics to be pseudo-statements. (Carnap 1959: 60–61, *emphasis* in the original)

Following the Wittgensteinian thesis that the meaning of a sentence is the method of its verification,[42] logical positivists proposed verificationism as the main criterion of demarcation between science and metaphysics.[43] The thought, in simple words, was that where empirical verification, including in-principle verification, is not possible, we are not dealing with science but with metaphysics. Notoriously verificationism, both as a demarcation criterion as well as a constraint on meaning, encountered insurmountable objections chief among which was the failure to classify as scientific all kinds of universally quantified generalizations. This is of course a major shortcoming since many statements that we would certainly classify as scientific take the form of a universal quantification (e.g., the statement that all electrons are negatively charged). However, statements like these cannot be verified, since a verification for such claims would require a method for checking every instance of the generally quantified statement, which is clearly not feasible (and in certain cases not even possible). Another problematic set of cases is given by negative existential generalizations (statements such as "there exists no sphere of uranium with a diameter of 1 mile" or "there is no phlogiston in nature"). All these statements

---

[42] For a very recent revised and precisified version of the verifiability criterion for the meaningfulness of declarative sentences, see Leitgeb (2023).

[43] Wittgenstein is generally interpreted as conceiving of this thesis primarily as a constitutive principle of meaning as discussed in his *Tractatus Logico-Philosophicus*.

would be classified as non-scientific, which is evidently an unacceptable consequence of the verificationist criterion of demarcation since these are clearly true scientific statements.

After this first, important but ultimately unsuccessful, attempt, the discussion of demarcation was then taken up by Karl Popper who, like the logical positivists, was highly invested in the quest of devising a strict criterion for distinguishing science from non-science. As a matter of fact he thought that demarcating science from non-science constituted the "key to most of the fundamental problems in the philosophy of science" (Popper 1962: 42). Popper rejected the logical positivists' idea that verifiability provides the demarcation criterion and suggested falsifiability instead. The thought was that in order to count as scientific a theory must issue predictions which should be capable of conflicting with possible or conceivable observation – that is, for any scientific theory or hypothesis it should be possible to come up with observations which would prove the theory or hypothesis wrong (see Popper 1962: 39). Moreover, Popper made it clear that the kind of falsifiability referred to in his demarcation criterion "only has to do with the logical structure of sentences and classes of sentences" (Popper [1989] 1994: 82). In this respect, a theoretical statement (a prediction) is falsifiable if and only if it logically contradicts some (empirical) statement about a possible observable event, where the modality involved is logical modality (Popper [1989] 1994: 83). It's worth noticing that Popper's falsification procedure takes the form of a modus tollens: roughly, a recalcitrant observation entails the negation of the working hypothesis. Thus, Popper's demarcation criterion heavily relies on the validity of certain logical principles (in particular modus tollens, and, more fundamentally, modus ponens and absurdum).

Popper's account was criticized on several counts. A principled criticism came from considerations related to the so-called Duhem-Quine thesis according to which theoretical hypotheses cannot be directly falsified by recalcitrant observations, since they only entail observation-statements when taken together with auxiliary hypotheses. Thus, when observations do not accord with the predictions of the targeted theoretical hypothesis we face a choice: either you reject (or amend) the hypothesis (and thus the theory) or you reject (or amend) at least some of the auxiliary hypotheses. A second principled set of criticism points to a misclassification issue in that it seems to rule out what are widely, but perhaps controversially, considered legitimate sciences (such as psychology and sociology) while classifying what we intuitively would consider pseudosciences (e.g., astrology) as scientific.[44] For example, many psychological

---
[44] On this issue see Laudan (1983), Agassi (1991), Hansson (2006).

theories deal with complex human behavior, which is influenced by numerous, sometimes non-quantifiable factors, making strict falsification difficult. Similarly, sociological theories often aim to understand broad social patterns that are challenging to test in controlled, falsifiable experiments. In contrast, astrologists may formulate rather bold predictions about individual behaviors or events, which could then be tested and potentially falsified in a rather straightforward way. A third, more specific, set of issues, shared with verificationism, concerns negative existential generalizations which were classified as unscientific in Popper's account. Despite these difficulties, Popper's influence within the scientific community was so prominent for many years that even contemporary discussions of the scientific status of certain theories (e.g., string theory) make implicit reference to some form of falsificationist ideas.[45]

Imre Lakatos carried forward the quest for a precise demarcation criterion, refining the approach initially proposed by Popper by means of what he labeled "sophisticated (methodological) falsificationism." While Lakatos believed there was merit in Popper's approach to demarcation, he was critical of several key aspects of it. In particular, he considered Popper's view too restrictive since it predicts that a big part of everyday scientific practice is unscientific – which is arguably an unwelcome result. He thus proposed a somewhat radical revision of Popper's account. Let's briefly explore the key differences between Lakatos' and Popper's approaches to the demarcation of science.

For one thing, Lakatos, differing from Popper, adopted a more holistic approach to the demarcation issue. He suggested that the demarcation criterion should not be applied to an isolated hypothesis, statement, or theory, but rather considered in a broader context. More specifically, in applying the demarcation criterion we should take into account entire research programs which are characterized as a series of theories with a common hard core of fundamental ideas and a shared set of methodological rules. The hard core is enclosed by a protective belt of auxiliary hypotheses, observation statements as well as statements describing initial and boundary conditions. The methodological rules guide the research within a research program by means of a positive and a negative heuristic. The positive heuristic directs researchers toward fruitful avenues of inquiry, suggesting paths to explore. Conversely, the negative heuristic advises which paths should be avoided in conducting research. While the hard core is irrefutable by fiat, what goes into the protective belt can always be changed with the aim of safeguarding the core of the program. This led Lakatos to give up falsifiability as the sole demarcation criterion which

---

[45] As suggested by the title of Peter Woit's book, *Not Even Wrong: The Failure of String Theory and the Search for Unity in Physical Law* (see Woit 2006).

can effectively discriminate between science and non-science. In principle a research program can be falsifiable, in some sense of the term, but qualify, intuitively, as unscientific, and, conversely, a research program can be scientific but unfalsifiable. In opposition to Popper, Lakatos believed that it is permissible to protect the core of a research program from empirical refutation. Additionally, Lakatos had a more lenient approach to demarcation compared to Popper in another vital aspect: he did not view the discovery of an inconsistency within a research program as a definitive reason for condemning a research program as unscientific. As Lakatos puts the point: "The discovery of an inconsistency – or of an anomaly – [need not] immediately stop the development of a programme: it may be rational to put the inconsistency into some temporary, ad hoc quarantine, and carry on with the positive heuristic of the programme" (Lakatos 1978: 58).

Equipped with these insights, Lakatos offers a more flexible framework for demarcation, effectively aligning the criteria for what constitutes science with the characteristics of a good (i.e., progressive) scientific program. A research program is assessed as progressive if the old theories are subsequently replaced with new theories which, while preserving the same core theses, predict novel and hitherto unexpected facts, some of which are then confirmed by observation. Given this, contrary to Popper's dogmatic approach, Lakatos deemed it as rational to ignore anomalies so long as a research program is progressing. On the contrary, a research program is considered degenerating if its successive theories do not yield novel predictions or if the new predictions they do offer are proven false. This distinction underscores the dual importance of theoretical innovation and empirical validation in evaluating the scientific merit of a research program. In this way the science–pseudoscience spectrum sees an internal articulation that ranges from highly progressive research programs at one end of the spectrum to highly degenerative ones at the other.

Undoubtedly, Lakatos' proposal effectively improved on Popper's account of demarcation. In particular, it gives us a more realistic picture of demarcation than what is delivered by Popper's account. Moreover, it helped significantly in dealing with the problematic aspect of falsificationism as the sole demarcation criterion, especially with the issue of negative existential generalizations that were treated as unscientific in Popper's model.

However, despite its numerous merits, Lakatos' proposal is not immune to criticisms. In their critical piece on Lakatos' "The Methodology of Scientific Research Programme" (in Lakatos 1978), Catherine Elgin and Jonathan Adler (Elgin & Adler 1980) put forward a series of criticisms to Lakatos' account of demarcation. For one thing, they object that Lakatos made real progress over Popper in relation to the search for a demarcation criterion. They write: "The distinction between progressive and degenerating problemshifts is a distinction between good and bad science (or perhaps, promising and unpromising science). It cannot solve the original problem of differentiating science from non-science" (Elgin & Adler 1980: 414).

Moreover, they put forward a series of criticisms to Lakatos' idea that the hard core of a scientific program is practically irrefutable by empirical evidence. The core of the criticism lies in the realization that while "fallibilism constrains us to recognize that when we take evidence to count against the hard core of a programme we may be wrong [...] it does not compel us to conclude that evidence can never tell against the hard core" (Elgin & Adler 1980: 416). As a matter of fact, the criticism goes, we cannot exclude that after careful investigation we are forced to conclude that none of the auxiliary hypotheses in the protective belt is wrong. But, if that turns out to be the case, we would be forced to conclude that something in the hard core is wrong.

A second influential line of criticism comes from William Newton-Smith who has argued that Lakatos' proposal is theoretically wanting because it leaves out important conceptual aspects of science in the evaluation of what counts as a progressive (and thus good) research program. The concern, according to Newton-Smith, is that "[A]ny model of science must leave room for the differential assessment of theories in terms of their power to avoid conceptual difficulties and not just in terms of their power to predict novel facts and explain known facts" (Newton-Smith 1981: 89).

This is an important shortcoming for a demarcation criterion that has the ambition to be fully comprehensive and adequate not only in demarcating science from non-science but also in distinguishing good science from bad science. In this respect not even Lakatos' highly refined proposal was deemed sufficiently accurate to provide a sharp and univocal demarcation criterion.

Due to the numerous unsuccessful attempts to establish a clear and practical criterion for demarcation, skepticism about the feasibility of the project began to spread within the community of philosophers of science. In particular, the search for a demarcation criterion lost much of its traction after Larry Laudan's 1983 paper "The Demise of the Demarcation Problem." In this critical piece, Laudan severely doubted the philosophical significance of searching for a demarcation criterion claiming that the question – what makes a theory scientific? – "is both uninteresting and, judging by its checkered past, intractable" (Laudan 1983: 125). At the core of his argument is the thought that given the "epistemic heterogeneity of the activities and beliefs customarily regarded as scientific," searching for a demarcation criterion is a futile quest. He proposed instead to focus on the question: What makes a belief well founded (or heuristically fertile)? – which he considered both philosophically interesting and tractable. This approach effectively shifts our investigation from the specific field of philosophy of science to a broader inquiry encompassing insights from both epistemology and cognitive psychology.

For a few decades Laudan's skepticism toward the search for a demarcation criterion dominated the scene in the philosophy of science and thus what Popper considered one of the core issues in the discipline was, for better or worse, mostly ignored. More recently, philosophical discussions over demarcating science from non-science (including pseudoscience) made a comeback.[46] The new impulse to the debate on demarcation sprang from the basic thought that having some indication on how to distinguish scientific from non-scientific theories and discipline not only remains a reasonable and perhaps philosophically interesting endeavor but it also has quite significant implications for our society. Consider, for instance, the enormous impact that scientific results have, directly or indirectly, on policy makers, education, as well as decisions concerning the distribution of research fundings.[47] When deciding between funding medical or naturopathic research, governments need criteria to justify preferring the former over the latter. This preference could be based on the understanding that medical research, unlike naturopathic research, is scientifically grounded. Another prominent reason for the importance of a philosophical investigation on the issue of demarcation concerns the broad phenomenon of science denialism which is due, for a significant part, to a profound mistrust in scientific institutions which is motivated primarily by some deep misunderstanding of what science is and how it works.

Be that as it may, in the 1970s and 1980s, a shift occurred from single to multicriteria approaches.[48] Historically, multicriteria approaches to the demarcation issue can be traced back to the work of Karl Gustav Hempel and Thomas Kuhn,[49] and have been more recently (and explicitly) advocated by Sven Hansson and Martin Mahner,[50] among others. In general, the post-Laudan science-demarcation trend[51] has relaxed the demands for what should count as philosophically interesting and practically useful demarcation criteria either by dropping the strict project of isolating a set of individually necessary and jointly sufficient criteria for scientificity or by supplementing such a strict

---

[46] See, Blancke, Boudry, and Pigliucci (2017); Boudry (2022); Dawes (2018); Hansson (2020); Hirvonen and Karisto (2022); Holman and Wilholt (2022); Letrud (2019); McIntyre (2019).

[47] See Mahner (2013) and Hansson (2021) for a more detailed discussion.

[48] See, Bunge (1984), Radner & Radner (1982), Hansson (2013). See Hirvonen & Karisto (2022) for a discussion.

[49] See, Hempel (1951) and Kuhn (1977).

[50] See, Hansson (2021) and Mahner (2013).

[51] See, especially, Pigliucci (2013), Hansson (2013), Mahner (2013).

definition with a set of additional criteria which are discipline-specific in order to become fully operative. Multicriteria approaches to demarcation can be articulated in a variety of ways. In one articulation, generally speaking, the primary task of a multicriteria approach is to come up with a list of features (arguably a stratified list with some primary and some secondary elements) that a discipline has to satisfy in order to count as a scientific discipline. This set of features should be strict and precise enough to leave out any discipline that we would confidently judge not to be a science and, on the other hand, general and malleable enough to be able to capture the important variety of special sciences. Quite predictably, there will be controversial cases and the decision about those may require appealing to some extra factors. In a somewhat more flexible interpretation of the multicriteria approach, determining whether a theory T qualifies as scientific involves checking if it meets any of the agreed-upon sufficient conditions, or if it fails to meet any of the necessary conditions for being considered scientific. Sebastian Lutz seems to suggest something in this ballpark when he criticizes Laudan's claim that "without conditions which are both necessary and sufficient, we are never in a position to say this is scientific: but that is unscientific" (Laudan 1983: 119). Lutz in fact argues: "But Laudan's claim is false: To be able to say that a is scientific (Sa) while b is not ($\neg Sb$), all that is needed is one sufficient condition ϕ that is fulfilled by a [...] and one necessary condition ψ that is not fulfilled by b [...]. Laudan's demand that ϕ and ψ be one and the same is supererogatory" (Lutz 2011: 126)

In a recent paper, Ilmari Hivonen and Janne Karisto go even further and claim:

> Even though Lutz is clearly right, we are willing to take one step further: criteria of either type would already suffice for making demarcations and, perhaps, neither are needed. If we have necessary conditions of science – without sufficient ones – we can judge as untrustworthy those epistemic projects that claim to be scientific but do not meet the conditions. [...] The same holds if we are endowed with sufficient conditions [...] If the proper sciences meet the sufficient conditions of science, whereas the pseudosciences do not, it seems obvious which group should be trusted. Thus, merely sufficient conditions of science would already be very welcome. (Hirvonen & Karisto 2022: 714)

We agree that traditional approaches to the demarcation problem based on finding a set of necessary and sufficient conditions have little chances of success. For this reason, we will adhere to the recent trend of considering a multicriteria approach to demarcation as the most promising framework to effectively demarcate science from non-science. Our proposal is to adopt, within a multicriteria approach, an abductivist model concerning theory choice according to which rival theories are chosen on the basis of their score in relation to a variety of factors (or, more aptly, theoretical virtues). Many are the theoretical virtues proposed and discussed in the literature. However, given the somewhat restricted scope of our project, we will focus on discussing those core criteria that seem relevant for assessing the scientificity of logic (which, intuitively, may well be among the controversial cases). Core demarcation criteria that have been discussed in the literature include generality, empirical adequacy, revisability on the basis of (possibly empirical) evidence, explanatory power, predictive success, modeling capacity, and amenability to the use of abductive methods for theory choice – in particular, scientific strength and simplicity. A further important criterion which is typically omitted in discussion about demarcation and theory choice criteria – a *glaring* omission, as Gila Sher would put it[52] – is truth. While this list isn't exhaustive, it is nonetheless representative of the most important demarcation criteria within a multicriteria approach. Furthermore, while there are different methods for weighing and aggregating these criteria, we will not take a definitive position on this issue in this volume. Instead, in Section 5, we will offer a concise overview of these criteria, applying them to address the question: Is logic a science? Section 4 will delve into the subject of demarcation in logic.

4 Demarcation in Logic

The term "logic" may have a variety of different uses. For instance, "logic," in its broad sense, could be used to refer to the discipline of logic as practiced by logicians with, arguably, its distinctive subject matter (or subject matters); or, more narrowly, it could be employed to refer to a certain formal system (e.g., classical first-order logic with identity); or, even more narrowly, it could be used to refer to a specific application, as in *the logic of rice-cookers*. We take it that the demarcation issue concerns primarily the task of separating the discipline of logic in its own right from other disciplines (as with the sciences, the task is to demarcate a scientific discipline, e.g., physics, from non-scientific disciplines, e.g., astrology).

In order to make progress on this task we need to get a grip on how to conceive of the subject matter of logic, at least for the limited purposes of this project. First of all, we are here interested exclusively in what is traditionally called *deductive logic* – we will thus ignore the large variety of non-deductive logics. Moreover, for the sake of simplifying things we will mostly focus on first order logic as the paradigmatic case, even though our discussion should be taken to be generalizable to the various extensions of first-order logic

---

[52] Personal conversation.

(higher-order logics, modal logics, temporal logics, etc.). In this respect, what we have in mind with the expression *the discipline of logic* is the kind of discipline which concerns deductive logic. Clearly this only covers one part – albeit, traditionally, the prominent part – of the general discipline of logic which should be thought of as encompassing a broader variety of logics (both deductive and non-deductive). The main reason for restricting our attention to the deductive family of logics – besides the prosaic reason of the limited space at our disposal – is that current debates on logical anti-exceptionalism are mostly focused on deductive logic(s) and thus we follow that thread.

With this in hand, we should now ask: how do we go about identifying the discipline of (deductive) logic? A first sensible step toward addressing this question is to get a grip on what (deductive) logic is about (in a sense, an attempt to fix the referent of the term "logic"). The way we will go about this will be to ask whether logic has a distinctive subject matter. In a partially ecumenical spirit, and broadly speaking, we may say that logic studies a special set of formal features, that could be taken to be (the most general) features of the world (and thus objectual) or features concerning certain types of arguments or inferences framed in a suitably regimented language (and thus linguistic or meta-linguistic). Following the objectual thread, one could take logic to concern primarily (a distinctive, but not necessarily special category of) truths about the mostly non-linguistic world (e.g., formal truths). Following the, perhaps more traditional and widespread, linguistic (or meta-linguistic) thread, we could take logic to be primarily about validity – what logically follows from what.[53] For illustrative purposes, we will here take the discipline of logic to be primarily about validity, even though what we will say about demarcation generalizes smoothly to objectual interpretations of the primary subject matter of logic.[54] In so doing, we will discuss two broad attempts to provide a demarcation criterion in logic, one belonging to the so-called model-theoretic tradition and the other belonging to the so-called proof-theoretic tradition.

According to the conception of *logic-as-the-science-of-validity*, the chief task of logic is to study what follows from what and to provide systematic explanations about why certain sentences (or propositions) follow from some other sentences (or propositions). Validity is a property of arguments which is generally introduced by means of the notion of consequence: an argument is valid just

---

[53] At this level of generality, we are not committing to any specific account of validity (whether model-theoretic or proof-theoretic, classical, non-classical, or pluralistic, etc.).

[54] For at least for some of those who hold the objectual approach (e.g., Penelope Maddy and Gila Sher), the objectual approach just is the validity approach. However, some other philosophers (e.g., Timothy Williamson), keep the two approaches sharply distinct.

in case the conclusion follows from (is a consequence of) the premises.[55] There are many ways of evaluating arguments. We are here concerned with deductive logic, and thus with the notion of *logical validity* (and *logical consequence*). It is thus pivotal to clarify what is meant by these notions.

The task of providing a neat characterization of logical validity is not an easy one.[56] Coming from the study of the semantics of natural language one may be prone to take seriously our (as competent users of the language, perhaps with some degree of idealization) judgments about what intuitively follows from what. Within the philosophy of logic debate, a clear example of this attitude is provided by Graham Priest who writes: "It is clear enough what provides the data in the case of an empirical science: observation and experiment. What plays this role in logic? The answer, I take it, is our intuitions about the validity or otherwise of vernacular inferences" (Priest 2016: 355).

This view relies on the assumption that there is a pre-theoretical conception of validity which provides the chief adequacy criterion for the characterization of logical validity and logical consequence. This assumption can be doubted on the basis of three main considerations. First, it could be argued that the notions of logical validity, as well as that of logical truth, are fairly technical notions on which folk's intuitions have no special jurisdiction. As Gil Sagi aptly points out: "The concept here, logical consequence, is importantly different from other basic philosophical concepts such as justice and beauty, in that it is predominantly a theoretical concept. Discussions on what is logical consequence and even the mere use of the concept hardly occur outside academic contexts, with the outcome that its study may be especially insulated" (Sagi: Forthcoming).

One may object that the kind of relevant data here are not intuitions targeting directly validity, which is indeed a technical concept, but judgments concerning the correctness of instances of inferences in reasoning using natural language. These are taken to be somewhat a reliable indication of the targeted phenomenon, namely validity. However, the reliability of these judgments is highly contestable: folk are typically bad in reliably assessing which arguments are valid and which are not.[57] Second, even focusing on the intuitions of logically trained folk we find a significant degree of diversity that challenges a unified

---

[55] Proof-theoretically, given a certain proof-system PF, an argument from a set of premises Gamma to a conclusion C is valid (according to PF) if there is a derivation of C from Gamma (a derivation made only of steps licensed by rules of PF and all of whose undischarged assumptions are either axioms of the proof-systems or members of Gamma).

[56] Here, we treat the notions of validity and logical consequence as interchangeable.

[57] As evidenced by the famous "Selection Task" ideated by Peter Wason (1966) which shows that a large majority of agents cannot solve an abstract reasoning task involving conditionals. See Kahneman (2011) for a comprehensive discussion, and Tajer (forthcoming) for a critical take on the matter.

pre-theoretic conception of validity. Third, appealing to pre-theoretical intuitions about logical validity is bound to give predictions that logicians would typically regard as incorrect. In fact, there are arguments that we may intuitively consider valid, in some pre-theoretic sense of *valid*, but which arguably fail to count as valid in the strict (logicians) sense of logically valid. Take for instance the following one-premise arguments:

(*) Julia's car is red, therefore Julia's car is colored.

(**) Karl is a bachelor, therefore Karl is a male.

(***) The stuff in the glass is water; therefore, the stuff in the glass is H_2O.

In all three cases it would certainly be correct to claim that the conclusion follows from the premise. In fact, these arguments satisfy what is taken to be the core element behind the intuitive notion of *following from* – namely, a kind of preservation of truth from the premise to the conclusion with a strong guarantee: if the premises are true and the conclusion follows from the premises, the conclusion is guaranteed to be true. Notice that the kind of guarantee that we get in (*) and (**) is traditionally cashed out in terms of analyticity – that is, merely in virtue of how the terms "red" and "colored" in (*) and "bachelor" and male in (**) are defined – while the kind of guarantee that we get in (***), under standard Kripkean assumptions, is that of metaphysical necessity. This means that the sense of validity involved in these arguments is that of truth preservation guaranteed either in virtue of meaning (which can be thought of in terms of a kind of semantic necessity),[58] or in virtue of metaphysics.[59]

The question is whether they are valid in the logical sense – that is, where the truth of the conclusion follows from the truth of the premises with a kind of guarantee which is different (and supposedly stricter) than a conceptual and/or metaphysical guarantee. A quick reflection on these arguments shows that the sense of validity at issue there is not the strictest one that we can come up with. If we change the meaning of "red," and that of "colored" in the first argument, and the meaning of "bachelor" and that of "male" in the second argument, we can easily end up with arguments with true premises and a false conclusion. And the kind of guarantee that we get in the third argument very much depends on

---

[58] For those who do not like the notion of analyticity, the point can be restated using concepts and conceptual necessity instead.

[59] If modal monism is true, then either some of these claims are not necessary, or they are all necessary in the same (perhaps metaphysical) sense. In this section, we do not assume the truth of modal monism. Instead, we adopt a perspective that is compatible with, and perhaps even favorable to, modal pluralism (see Fine 2002 for a discussion of modal pluralism).

the widely accepted, but not completely uncontroversial, assumption that there are a posteriori necessities.[60]

This fact points to an important desideratum: what is required from an adequate characterization of the notion of logical validity is indifference or insensitivity to variations in the subject matter that the sentences involved in the argument are about. The idea is to look at the elements of the argument that remain unaffected by the variation in subject matter: this leaves us with the invariant structure of the argument – what is generally referred to as the *logical form*. What, in turns, determines what forms are logical are ultimately logical expressions. Consequently, what is ultimately needed to demarcate logic from other disciplines is a criterion of logicality on the basis of which we can sharply distinguish logical from non-logical expressions. We can thus determine which arguments are valid on the basis of the meaning of logical expressions alone. This desideratum for a criterion of logicality has a long history and it was explicitly endorsed by three key figures in the history of logic, namely Kant, Frege, and Tarski. The idea is, roughly, that a logically valid argument remains so regardless of how we interpret the non-logical terms occurring in a sentence. Once we have singled out the logical vocabulary – the logical constants of the language, thus expressions such as "and," "or," "not," "if ... then ..., " "for every ..., " "there exists ... " – and once we have settled on an interpretation of the logical vocabulary,[61] we can change the interpretation of anything else in the sentences involved in an argument without that having any effect on the question of whether the arguments are logically valid or not: if the argument transmits truth from the premises to the conclusion it will continue to do so regardless of how we reinterpret the non-logical expressions in the sentences.

In order to generate an adequate relation of logical consequence we need to delimit the class of logical constants as neatly as possible. The logical expressions determine the form of an argument which in turn ground its logical validity. We then get the following picture: arguments are (logically) valid in virtue of their *logical form*, which they have in virtue of the occurrence and

---

[60] Clearly, the kind of validity that can be defined within a modal extension of first-order logic will be effectively a deductive kind of validity since there are ways of extending first-order alethic logic into, for example, quantified modal logic, which preserve logicality.

[61] As Tarski points out, "Underlying our whole construction is the division of all terms of the language discussed into logical and extra-logical. [...] This division is certainly not quite arbitrary. If, for example, we were to include among the extra-logical signs the implication sign, or the universal quantifier, then our definition of the concept of consequence would lead to results which obviously contradict ordinary usage. On the other hand, no objective grounds are known to me which permit us to draw a sharp boundary between the two groups of terms. It seems to be possible to include among logical terms some which are usually regarded by logicians as extra-logical without running into consequences which stand in sharp contrast to ordinary usage" (Tarski 1936: 418).

distribution of the logical expressions in them. So, if we solve the demarcation issue at the level of the logical expressions (i.e., logical constants, quantifiers, etc.), we are thereby in a position to determine which arguments have the proper form which guarantees preservation of truth from premises to conclusion.

Aligned with what is nowadays referred to as *the Tarskian tradition*,[62] what's distinctive about the notion of logical validity can be rendered in terms of its insensitivity to the identity of the referents of the non-logical expressions (or, equivalently, as an inability to discriminate an object from any other object on the basis of its properties).[63] This criterion is known as *permutation invariance*.[64] In Tarski's own words, logic is thus characterized as "the science which deals with the notions invariant under the widest class of transformations," which are notions "of a very general character" (Tarski 1986: 149).

Tarski's permutation invariance criterion of logicality was inspired by Felix Klein's work in the foundations of geometry (Klein 1872). Klein has shown how we can characterize geometries in terms of the group(s) of transformations under which their characteristic notions remain invariant. Let's consider, for instance, Euclidean geometry which, roughly, studies the shape of rigid bodies. A peculiar feature of shape is that it does not change when moving objects through space: for instance, the shape of a rectangular triangle does not change by rotating it by an arbitrary degree. This is because rotation is a kind of transformation that preserves the distance between points – that is, it is an isometric transformation.[65] More generally, Euclidean geometry is invariant not just under isometric transformations but under the broader group of similarity transformations: these include, in addition to isometric transformations, also transformations that preserve the ratio of distances between points – for example, a rectangular triangle remains a rectangular triangle even when it is

---

[62] This may not have been Tarski's preferred way of putting things, but we abstract here from exegetical issues. It should be pointed out, as evidenced by the quote from Tarski in the previous footnote, that in 1936 Tarski refrains from providing a demarcation criterion, leaving it open whether an objectively correct criterion of logicality could be found. However, Tarski returned to the question of logicality in a later lecture (Tarski 1986), where a unique demarcation criterion is proposed: logical constants are those kinds of expressions whose extensions remain constant under all permutations of individuals. Some philosophers have expressed skepticism about the possibility of finding a principled demarcation criterion. For instance, John Etchemendy (1990) and Stephen Read (1994) agree that validity is relative to a choice of logical constants and that no principled demarcation criterion of logicality can be found.

[63] See MacFarlane (2000) for a thorough discussion of three senses in which logic could be said to be formal.

[64] Starting from a set of objects S, a permutation, intuitively, is a kind of rearrangement of the members of the set. More precisely, a permutation P is a function from a set S to itself such that (i) no two distinct objects belonging to S are assigned the same value under P and (ii) every member of S is mapped to some object or other under P.

[65] Isometric transformations are: reflection, rotation, translation, and arbitrary combinations of them.

shrunk or enlarged uniformly. In this sense, Euclidean geometry can be characterized as the study of shape properties that remain unaffected by similarity transformations. By increasing the group(s) of transformations under which geometrical notions remain invariant, Klein has shown how to classify geometries by means of their generality: the intuitive connection here is that the higher the number of transformations that a notion is invariant under, the more general the notion is – and consequently the geometry to which it belongs. For instance, affine geometry can be thought to be more general than Euclidean geometry because its notions are invariant under a broader group of transformations, transformations preserving lines and parallelism, which properly include the similarity transformations.

There are many types of invariance. According to Gila Sher, who is nowadays one of the leading proponents of the Tarskian approach, the kind of invariance that is taken to be relevant for the demarcation issue in logic involves properties and individuals not only within one set or domain, but across (equinumerous) domains. Thus, Sher generalizes Tarski's permutation invariance criterion of logicality into an isomorphism invariance: in this sense we speak of invariance under a 1–1 and onto replacement of individuals (within and across domains). Let's briefly see what this means. Every property is invariant under some 1–1 and onto replacement of individuals – trivially, every property is invariant under the identity replacement of individuals. But many properties are also invariant in a nontrivial way – their degree of nontriviality being proportional to their degree of generality. To use an example given by Gila Sher:

> [T]he first-level property is-a-human distinguishes between Tarski and Mount Everest, but not between Tarski and (Meryl) Streep or between Everest and the number 1. You can replace Tarski by Streep or Everest by 1 and the property is-a-human will not notice. But if you replace Tarski by Everest (or 1), it will. This can be expressed in terms of "invariance": is-a-human is invariant under replacements of Tarski by Streep and of Everest by 1, but not under replacements of Tarski or Streep by Everest or 1. (Sher 2022: 31)

We can construct other examples that demonstrate an increasingly higher degree of generality. The interesting question is whether there are properties that are invariant under *all* replacements of individuals (under all isomorphisms, or bijections) – that is, whether there are *maximally invariant* properties. According to what is known as the Tarski-Sher thesis, these properties exist and they are the logical properties. Seen in this way, the logical notions can be thought of as the limit point of a chain of progressively more abstract (more formal) notions defined by their invariance under wider groups of permutations (isomorphisms) of domains. This provides, according to Sher, a neat and general solution to the demarcation issue in logic:

> (Tarski–Sher Thesis) – A property is logical iff it is invariant under all isomorphisms (it is invariant under all bijections, it is maximally invariant).[66]

This criterion gives us an explanation of the kind of systematicity and strict modal force proper of the notion of logical consequence. In fact, it is taken to reliably characterize all and only properties/constants that give rise to necessary and formal consequences as logical. Moreover, one important virtue of this approach is its flexibility. We can extend the set of logical constants/expressions by stipulating that a certain set of expressions should be kept invariant. For instance, if we are interested in investigating the structure of time, we can add temporal operators to the set of logical constants, thus keeping their interpretation fixed. The same goes for different kinds of modal operators.

Sher's improvement on Tarski's logicality criterion is, to this date, arguably the most refined criterion of logicality offered within the model-theoretic conception of logical consequence. As MacFarlane points out:

> As an account of the distinctive generality of logic, then, [it] has much to recommend it. It is philosophically well-motivated and mathematically precise, it yields results that accord with common practice, and it gives determinate rulings about some borderline cases (for example, set-theoretic membership). Best of all, it offers hope for a sharp and principled demarcation of logic that avoids cloudy epistemic and semantic terms like "about," "analytic," and "a priori." (MacFarlane 2017)

There are nevertheless limitations to this approach.[67] For one thing, it does not completely solve the worry of overgeneralization: this criterion would classify as logical some expressions, like finite and infinite cardinality quantifiers, that (at least some) logicians would not be willing to classify as logical.[68] Moreover, and somehow conversely, a few authors have charged the test with undergenerating

---

[66] See Sher (2022: 37). Besides Sher (2022), see MacFarlane (2000) and Speitel (forthcoming) for a more detailed presentation and critical discussion of the Tarski-Sher thesis.

[67] See Bonnay (2014) for an overview of the various criticisms moved against the Tarski-Sher Thesis, as well as Sher (2016) and Griffiths and Paseau (2022) for discussion. See Sher (2022), Griffiths and Paseau (forthcoming), and Speitel (forthcoming) for further discussion. Additionally, an important question arises as to whether this approach can be extended to non-classical logics.

[68] Feferman (1999, 2010) criticize the isomorphism-invariance criterion because it classifies as logical finite and infinite cardinality quantifiers, while they are intuitively mathematical expressions. McGee puts forward a different kind of overgeneralization objection by concocting expressions, like the unicorn and H_2O negations, which are coextensive with generally accepted logical expressions, but which have non-logical meanings (see McGee 1996: 569). See Griffiths and Paseau (2022, Ch. 9) for a general strategy to counter the overgeneralization objection. See Sagi (2015) for a reply to McGee-style overgeneralization objections.

by classifying as logical too few logical constants.[69] Be that as it may, for the purposes of our project in this Element the Tarski-Sher Thesis offers us a useful and refined tool for demarcating the discipline of logic from other disciplines: logic is the discipline concerned with notions of maximal generality, that is, notions that are invariant under all 1–1 and onto replacements of individuals.

Efforts have also been made to establish an effective demarcation criterion in logic within the proof-theoretic tradition. Such an approach could be seen as more fine-grained, from an epistemological point of view, than the model theoretic one. The thought is roughly that proof theory is not interested exclusively in whether a certain conclusion C follows from a set of premises P1, ..., Pn, but also in the way we reach C starting from P1, ..., Pn. In this respect, as Kreisel pointed out, "Proofs and their representations by formal derivations are treated as principal objects of study, not as mere tools for analyzing the consequence relation."[70]

From a broad philosophical perspective, proof-theoretic approaches to logic belong to the semantic tradition called *inferentialism*. Inferentialism has its roots in the philosophy of the late Wittgenstein, who viewed the meaning of a term as explained by reference to the way in which it is used in our language (in the famous motto: the meaning of a word is its use in a language).[71] More specifically, the core idea behind the proof-theoretic approach to logic is that the meaning of logical constants is given by the role that these play within an inferential context (e.g., a formal or informal proof). The use of a logical constant is regimented by a set of purely inferential rules which come in two main varieties (right and left rules in Gentzen-style sequent calculi; introduction and elimination rules in Prawitz-style natural deduction systems),[72] and which correspond to two core aspects of meaning. As Dummett, in an oft-cited passage, makes clear:

> [T]here are always two aspects of the use of a given form of sentence: the conditions under which an utterance of that sentence is appropriate, which include, in the case of an assertoric sentence, what counts as an acceptable ground for asserting it; and the consequences of an utterance of it, which comprise both what the speaker commits himself to by the utterance and the appropriate response on the part of the hearer, including, in the case of assertion, what he is entitled to infer from it if he accepts it. (Dummett 1973: 396)

In other words, the first aspect of meaning of a logical connective $, which is reminiscent of a verificationist constraint on assertibility, specifies the

---

[69] See, for instance, Dutilh Novaes (2014), Woods (2014), and MacFarlane (2017).
[70] Kreisel (1971): 109. [71] Wittgenstein (2009): 25 (I, §43).
[72] See von Plato (2014) for a discussion of the development of proof theory.

circumstances under which an assertion/endorsement of a statement involving $ is licensed. The second aspect of meaning, which incorporates a pragmatist element, specifies what we can legitimately infer from a statement containing $ as the main connective in virtue of having asserted/endorsed it. To fully grasp the correct use of a logical connective, and thus its meaning, acquaintance with both aspects is needed (although each aspect may be strictly speaking sufficient to fully and uniquely determine the meaning of a sentence in which it occurs).

To get a proof-theoretically acceptable demarcation criterion between logical and non-logical expressions we need to provide a neat way of isolating the *purely inferential* rules from other seemingly suitable rules. As a matter of fact, not any set of inference rules will confer a stable and coherent meaning on the logical constants. We cannot be too permissive, as the (in)famous tonk operator devised by Arthur Prior shows.[73] Tonk is a connective which has the introduction rule of disjunction (which allows you to derive A tonk B from A) and the elimination rule of conjunction (that allows you to derive B from A tonk B). As it is easy to see, introducing this operator in a (non-trivial) formal system (defined as the set of operational and structural rules it permits) would have a hugely disruptive effect on our existing inferential practice allowing us to derive everything from anything (non-empty set of premises).[74] This is why Prior labeled it a *runabout inference ticket*.

How can we make sure that seemingly logical connectives like tonk do not qualify as logical? The standard response is to appeal to the so-called notion of harmony. The intuitive idea behind harmony is that the introduction and elimination rules of a logical connective need to display a certain balance. More precisely, the introduction and elimination rules for an arbitrary logical connective $ cannot be determined independently of one another. The assertibility conditions of a sentence S containing $ as its main connective should be appropriately counterbalanced by the consequences a subject is thereby licensed to draw upon endorsement of S. In the case of tonk, the failure to qualify as a logical connective, although it closely mimics the behavior of a logical connective, is that in endorsing A tonk B by introducing it from some warranted proposition A following the introduction rule of tonk, a reasoner is thereby in a position to obtain, by a simple application of the elimination rule of tonk, novel grounds for asserting B. In other words, the problem with tonk is that by means of a mere application of its introduction and

---

[73] Prior (1960).
[74] With the presence of, for example, conditional proof or reductio, full triviality follows.

elimination rules a subject is in a position to boost her epistemic situation by acquiring new information (and if *A* and *B* are empirical, we will be in a position to get new empirical information). However, especially in the case of empirical information, it seems absurd that by means of reasoning via the sole employment of a putatively logical operator a subject enhances her epistemic situation. In this sense the tonk rules are disharmonious, and as such they fail to characterize an admissible logical connective. One way of backing up the intuitive thought behind the notion of harmony that we have just sketched is by means of what Florian Steinberger has labeled *the principle of innocence*: "[I]t should not be possible, solely by engaging in deductive logical reasoning, to discover hitherto unknown (atomic) truths that we would have been incapable of discovering independently of logic" (Steinberger 2011: 619).

In this respect, according to Steinberger, the primary purpose of harmony is exactly to secure the innocence of logic. Steinberger's principle of innocence echoes a passage from Michael Dummett when he writes: "[I]t should not be possible, by first applying one of the introduction rules for c and then immediately drawing a consequence from the conclusion of that introduction rule by means of an elimination rule of which it is the major premiss, to derive from the premisses of the introduction rule a consequence that we could not otherwise have drawn" (Dummett 1991: 247–248).[75]

The discussion on harmony and the issue of whether harmony provides us with a clear cut criterion of logicality is rather complex and we are not here in a position to provide a sufficiently exhaustive and precise description of the state of the art on these matters.[76] One important concern, which is worth mentioning, though, is that contrary to what has been observed in relation to the Tarskian-inspired model-theoretic account of logicality based on isomorphism invariance, a proof-theoretic criterion of logicality based on the notion of

---

[75] This quote expresses the basic insight behind what is known in the literature as *levelling of local peaks* test for harmony. Notoriously this test is effective against what is known as E-strong disharmony (like the case of tonk where you can deduce by an application of tonk elimination more than what could have been deduced from the grounds of the introduction rule of tonk) but not against E-weak disharmony – these are cases where the introduction rules are excessively strong when compared to the corresponding elimination rules (as in the case of quantum disjunction). See Steinberger (2011) for a detailed discussion of these points.

[76] How to spell out harmony in a precise formal fashion is a rather complex issue on which there's ample debate: see, for instance Dummett (1991), Milne (1994), Read (2010), Steinberger (2011), Tennant (1997), and Tranchini (2016). Moreover, what is the outcome of a harmony-based criterion of demarcation may depend on the format of the calculus (if it allows for multiple conclusions or just single conclusion) the structural assumptions characterizing the calculus (e.g., weakening, contraction, commutativity, associativity), and the format of the operational rules of the calculus (natural deduction versus sequent calculus). As Speitel notices, "this might be taken to introduce an unwelcome presentation-dependency into the determination of logicality" (Speitel forthcoming).

harmony is less flexible. There are notorious difficulties in extending a harmony-based criterion of logicality to modal notions.[77]

Be that as it may, and despite the potential divergence in results between the model-theoretic and the proof-theoretic accounts of logicality briefly discussed in this section, we can safely assume that there is some important overlap in outcome between these two broad criteria – an overlap which grants us a basic set of connectives that most logicians would be happy to consider properly logical regardless of their church: for example, the basic connectives and the elementary quantifiers "there is" and "for all." Whether this would suffice for singling out univocally and fully a logic is a matter of controversy. But we hope this brief discussion provides us with a sufficient grip on how to individuate (deductive) logic, at least as it is commonly conceived by philosophers and philosophical logicians, and thus to demarcate the discipline of logic from other disciplines.

5 Logic and Science: A Multicriteria Approach

5.1 Core Elements for the Comparison between Logic and Science

Thus far, we have examined approaches for distinguishing, on the one hand, the discipline of logic from other fields and, on the other hand, differentiating scientific disciplines from non-scientific ones. While we haven't arrived at definitive conclusions about demarcation (as previously mentioned, that is not among the aims of this Element), we have nevertheless gathered sufficient elements to advance our project. Specifically, we can now discuss what it takes for logic, as a discipline, to share enough characteristics with paradigmatic scientific disciplines, such as biology, chemistry, and physics, to be reasonably considered a science in its own right. Recognizing the difficulty of establishing a strict demarcation criterion based on necessary and sufficient conditions, we will adopt a multicriterial approach. Specifically, we will utilize the criteria outlined at the end of Section 3. Let us begin with a brief recap of these criteria and their relevance to logic.

Let's start with the ***truth*** criterion. A fundamental assumption of any scientific discipline is that it engages in truth-apt discourse. In other words, the statements that make up a scientific theory are intended to express truth-apt contents (propositions). Furthermore, truth is taken to play two distinct, albeit interconnected, normative functions in relation to scientific enquiry. On the one hand, truth is the aim of scientific inquiry in the sense that any specific scientific discipline is in the business of discovering truths about the world. On the other

---

[77] On this issue see Read (2008) and Steinberger (2009).

hand, truth is the chief criterion for assessing the correctness of our scientific inquiries in the sense that a scientific statement is correct just in case it expresses a true proposition.[78] How substantive these normative functions that truth exerts on scientific inquiries are will depend on a set of issues pertaining, on the one hand, on how to interpret the nature of truth and, on the other hand, how to understand the kind of normativity at issue.[79] Deciding on these issues will impact on the question of whether and to what extent logic satisfies the truth criterion. For instance, even if we grant that logical theories deal in truth-apt discourse (a view that may be challenged by logical non-cognitivists and logical expressivists), if we endorse some form of substantive correspondentist account of the nature of truth which is the one that may be reasonable to assume in relation to scientific inquiries, things may look controversial in the case of logic. To claim that the truth of logical statements lies in their correspondence with facts commits to endorsing a contentious metaphysics of substantive logical facts (e.g., facts which are mind-independent and determine, in some causal or metaphysical sense, the truth of our logical statements). By contrast, if we adopt a minimalist conception of the nature of truth, things would look much less controversial but also perhaps less interesting in relation to the comparison between logic and science since satisfaction of the truth criterion would be rather cheap. In a minimalist conception, the nature of truth is relatively insubstantial, serving primarily logical and expressive functions, such as indirect endorsement and generalization.[80] There is no need, then, to postulate the existence of substantial logical facts or a metaphysical or causal relationship between logical facts and logical statements. This means that once the truth-aptness of logical statements is granted, logic would be uncontroversially considered a science according to the truth criterion under a minimalist view of truth and its normativity. By contrast, by adopting a correspondence account of truth it would be significantly more controversial to consider logic a science under the truth criterion.[81]

The second criterion to discuss is ***generality***. A scientific discipline worth its name aims at issuing true, law-like generalizations about the world. The degree of generalization will of course vary depending on which specific scientific discipline we are talking about: for instance, the kind of generalizations reached by research in fundamental physics presumably will be broader in scope than those reached via research in ornithology. In this respect, the generality criterion should not be seen as in tension with the thesis that different sciences may vary

---

[78] See Shah & Velleman (2005).
[79] On this see Ferrari (2022).
[80] See Horwich 1998.
[81] If we adopt a pluralist stance on the notion of correspondence, as in Sher (2023b), things may look less controversial.

in their degree of generality – a thesis that could in principle be reconciled with certain versions of scientific (and logical) particularism (see Payette & Wyatt 2018). This is because there's a principled distinction between two theses: the thesis that a certain science (e.g., logic) has an universal scope of application versus the thesis that a science, in relation with its proper subject matter, seeks for generality. While the former is incompatible with particularism (and perhaps, in general, also problematic when it comes to the natural sciences), the latter is perfectly compatible with particularism. The kinds of generalizations issued by logic are law-like, and, arguably, they are the most general ones. These could take the form of metalinguistic generalizations about validity facts, as it were, like in: all the arguments based on modus ponens are valid. Alternatively, they could take the form of objectual generalizations about very abstract general patterns in the mostly non-linguistic world like in: for any given fact F, either F obtains or F doesn't obtain. Thus, when it comes to generality logic, as individuated by either the model-theoretic or the proof-theoretic criteria, is on the side of the sciences (at least on many accounts of the metaphysics and epistemology of logic, both on the exceptionalists and the anti-exceptionalist camps).

Third we may consider *adequacy* (or, the ability of being confirmed by evidence) as a second feature of comparison. We may distinguish between two notions of adequacy: factual and empirical adequacy.[82] While empirical adequacy entails factual adequacy, the converse does not hold. Factual adequacy is the claim that the adequacy conditions of a logical theory depend on worldly facts which are not necessarily empirical. Empirical adequacy is the stronger claim that the adequacy conditions of a logical theory depend on strictly empirical facts. What is the relationship between facts and empirical facts is a matter of controversy which depends on complex issues in the metaphysics of facts.[83] As it may be a matter of controversy whether the requirement of a logical theory to meet a factual adequacy criterion is itself already a challenge to an exceptionalist conception of logic. The adequacy conditions for paradigmatic sciences like physics, chemistry, and biology clearly require empirical adequacy. As a result, when considering the continuity between logic and the sciences in terms of adequacy, the notion of empirical adequacy becomes especially important. Therefore, we will focus on the criterion of empirical adequacy in the following discussion.

In general, empirical adequacy (which could be understood according to a variety of models like the hypothetico-deductive model, the inference to the

---

[82] We are grateful to Gila Sher for bringing this distinction to our attention.

[83] If one adopts a minimalist notion of facts, where referring to facts becomes relatively easy, then the requirement of factual adequacy also becomes rather cheap and not particularly distinctive of an anti-exceptionalist view of logic.

best explanation model, Bayesian models, etc.) is taken to be the primary ground for testing the success or unsuccess of a scientific theory (via confirmation or disconfirmation of its predictions). Claiming continuity between logic and science on the count of empirical adequacy is certainly more controversial than claiming continuity with respect to generality. What this would require is, at minimum, the thesis that logic is about aspects of the world that are empirically testable. Some proposals in this direction take the empirical data in logic to be considered judgments about which inferences formulated in the vernacular, as Priest has it, are acceptable (or good, or reasonable, etc.) and which aren't.[84] Another possibility would be to take data in logic to concern very general or structural features of the world which are somehow empirically detectable.[85] A third recognized source of empirical evidence within the purview of logic is data about language use. If one of the main tasks of logic as a discipline is that of formalizing natural language expressions in order to reveal (or disambiguate between) their logical form(s) then the linguistic judgments of competent users of the language may well count as empirical data. One case in point here is the debate about which one between material implication and relevant implication is more suitable to capture the way in which the expression "if ... then ... " is typically used in English.[86] In fact, relevant implication has been devised as an attempt to avoid the so-called paradoxes of material and strict implication.[87] An additional example is given by Penelope Maddy who takes the existence in the world of KF-structure[88] – namely, objects that enjoy and fail to enjoy properties, that stand and fail to stand in relations, where some situations involving these objects stand as ground to other situations as consequent – to exert a kind of evolutionary pressure on us which led to the development of a rudimentary logic of classical inferences involving conjunction, disjunction, negation, and quantification, capable of reliably tracking the structural features of the world.[89]

---

[84] These are generally *not* judgments about the validity of certain instances of a given logical principle (like modus ponens). As Hjortland and Martin aptly note: "the judgements of individuals over the correctness of arguments, or over whether some conclusion 'follows from' some premises, are treated as data and taken to be prima facie reliable indicators of validity. To interpret the content of the judgements as judgements about the validity of arguments would be to mistake the data with the phenomenon" (Martin & Hjortland 2021: 300).

[85] See Martin & Hjortland (2022), especially §4.2, for a discussion of these issues within their preferred *predictivist* framework.

[86] See Williamson (2020) for a (controversial) approach to understanding conditionals; see Bennett (2003) for a philosophical introduction to conditionals.

[87] These paradoxes are valid conclusions reached via the employment of material and strict implications but are assessed by competent users of natural language as highly controversial. See Anderson & Belnap (1975) and Dunn & Restall (2002).

[88] KF stands for Kant-Frege, and is used by Maddy to indicate (some of) Kant's forms of judgment, as improved by Frege's formal innovations – see Maddy (2014), chapter 3.

[89] See Maddy (forthcoming) and Maddy (2012).

A fourth feature that, as we have seen, is closely related to the second one, is the ***revisability on the basis of (empirical) evidence***. It is quite uncontroversial to claim that scientific theories whose predictions are in conflict with observation should be revised, possibly avoiding ad hoc amendments. Thus, revisability on the basis of empirical evidence is another hallmark of science. The applicability of this criterion to logical theories is an issue as contentious as the applicability of empirical confirmation to logic. In fact, it demands an analogous commitment to the idea that logic concerns empirically testable matters, as emphasized in the discussion of the previous criterion. The debate over the potential for empirical revisability probably reached its peak in the 1970s, particularly in relation to certain quantum phenomena that seem to require the revision of some principles of classical logic. More specifically, some philosophers, prominently Hilary Putnam,[90] have suggested in several papers that, given a certain interpretation of Heisenberg's uncertainty principle, the possibility of superposition in a quantum system requires the revision of classical distributivity principles (in particular, it requires the revision of the distributive principle of conjunction over disjunction).[91] Under the assumption that it makes as much sense to speak of "physical logic" as of "physical geometry," Putnam drew an analogy between the case of classical logic and quantum physics, and what happened to Euclidean geometry which was revised in light of its incompatibility with general relativity. Even though Putnam's argument did not find much agreement among logicians and philosophers of logic,[92] it offers an interesting case study to appreciate the possibility of empirical revisability of logic.

A fifth significant aspect relates to the ***explanatory power*** of a theory concerning the targeted phenomena. It is a hallmark of scientific disciplines to provide explanations of natural phenomena. The kind of phenomena may vary to a significant extent (perhaps, in tandem with the appropriate model of explanation),[93] depending on the specific science we are dealing with. For instance, while quantum physics provides explanations of natural phenomena at the atomic and subatomic scale, biology provides explanations of phenomena associated with living organisms and their vital processes. Does logic provide explanations? And if, so, what does logic explain? It seems reasonable to claim that logic is not in the business of providing causal explanations of natural phenomena. This already creates a stark contrast with the sciences, where causal

---

[90] See, especially, Putnam (1968).
[91] This is the classically valid principle $(p \wedge (q \vee r)) \equiv ((p \wedge q) \vee (p \wedge r))$.
[92] See Stairs (2016) as well as Kripke (2023).
[93] The thought being that different models of explanations (the deductive-nomological, the statistical, the causal, the mechanical, etc.) may be suitable for different scientific disciplines.

explanations are ubiquitous and of crucial importance. But there are other kinds of explanations that logical theories may offer. One natural option within the common understanding of logic as the science of validity is to say that logic does indeed explain facts about the validity or invalidity of arguments formulated in natural language.[94] This view is held, for instance, by Graham Priest:

> A decent logical theory is no mere laundry list of which inferences are valid/invalid, but also provides an explanation of these facts. (Priest 2016, 353)

And it is echoed by Payette and Wyatt:

> [W]hat we are looking to explain is the validity/invalidity of some argument consisting of (fully interpreted) natural language sentences. (Payette & Wyatt 2018: 159)

A different kind of explanatory role that logic may play has to do with providing informative generalizations which capture certain kind of observations of worldly state of affairs which we may call logical in character – for example, that either an object has a property or it lacks it; that if something is actually the case then it's also possible, and so on.

A sixth relevant criterion is ***amenability to be used as a modeling device***. Sciences make wide use of models which are thus taken to be of central importance in many scientific contexts. There are multiple kinds of models, but many scientific models are representational. Among well-known representational models in science we can mention the Watson and Crick three-dimensional double helix model of DNA, the billiard ball model of a gas, the Bohr model of the atom. Among others, Roy Cook, Michael Glanzberg, and Stewart Shapiro[95] take logic to align with the sciences in this respect: formal systems are taken to provide (mostly representational) models of targeted phenomena (phenomena arising, for instance, from natural language uses and reasoning). As Shapiro nicely puts it in his *Vagueness in Context*:

> The [...] claim is that a formal language is a mathematical model of a natural language, in roughly the same sense as, say, a Turing machine is a model of calculation, a collection of point masses is a model of a system of physical objects, and the Bohr construction is a model of an atom. In other words, a formal language displays certain features of natural languages, or idealizations thereof, while simplifying other features. (Shapiro 2006: 49)

A well-known example frequently discussed in the literature is the use of logic as a representational model for vagueness, a phenomenon widely regarded as

---

[94] It could be argued that logic also explains facts about the validity/invalidity of arguments formulated in, say, mathematics (including symbolic mathematics).
[95] See Cook (2000, forthcoming), Shapiro (2006, 2014), Glanzberg (2021).

pervasive in natural languages. In this context, we can employ precise mathematical tools to construct fruitful representations (i.e., models) of linguistic phenomena such as vagueness or any kinds of indeterminacies. By doing so we offer a way to represent and predict the behavior of vague terms without implying precision where it does not naturally exist.

Finally, in exploring the scientific standing of logic, another crucial factor is the methodological underpinnings of theory selection. It's commonly asserted that the choice of theories in science is predominantly guided by an **abductive methodology**, interpreted in a broad sense.[96] For instance, Williamson claims:

> We make the standard assumption that scientific theory choice follows a broadly abductive methodology. Scientific theories are compared with respect to how well they fit the evidence, of course, but also with respect to virtues such as strength, simplicity, elegance, and unifying power. We may speak loosely of inference to the best explanation, although in the case of logical theorems we do not mean specifically causal explanation, but rather a wider process of bringing our miscellaneous information under generalizations that unify it in illuminating ways. [...] The abductive methodology is the best science provides, and we should use it. (Williamson 2017: 334–335; see also Williamson 2013: 423–429)

To choose between rival scientific theories that exhibit comparable merits, particularly in terms of their explanatory and predictive power, scientists often rely on abductive criteria. These criteria include simplicity, non-adhocness, and strength. Some logicians, especially Ole Hjortland, Gillian Russell, and Timothy Williamson, following a broadly naturalist methodology coming from Quine, have argued that theory choice in logic should follow a similar abductive strategy. There are some core abductive criteria particularly useful to gain a better grasp of the extent to which an abductive methodology that works in the sciences can be carried over to the case of logic. Strength and simplicity are, in this perspective, paradigmatic ones. How should we understand these theoretical virtues?

Let us start with the notion of strength. A distinction can be drawn between logical and scientific strength.[97] In broad terms, the concept of a theory's logical strength concerns primarily the deductive power of the theory, while its scientific strength is largely related to the amount of informational content the theory delivers. More specifically, Williamson defines logical strength standardly as follows: "In one standard logical sense, a theory T is stronger than a theory T* if and only if T entails T* but T* does not entail T: every theorem of T* is

---

[96] See, especially, van Fraassen (1980), Lipton (2004), and Keas (2017).
[97] See Russell (2018) and Williamson (2017). The distinction can be traced back to van Fraassen, who distinguishes between logical and empirical strength – see van Fraassen (1980: 67–68).

a theorem of T, but not every theorem of T is a theorem of T*" (Williamson 2017: 336).[98]

Scientific strength, on the other hand, is standardly based on a notion of informativeness and specificity: scientifically stronger theories are more informative and specific. Indeed, they give better and more precise explanations. But what to make of this idea in the case of logic?[99] The thought is that a scientifically stronger logical theory is one that gives us more informative and precise answers to our questions – for example, questions like: does excluded middle hold for any sentence of our language? If not, for which sentences does it fail? Addressing questions like these can allow us to compare various logics – paradigmatically, classical and non-classical logics. Typically, non-classical logics restrict the range in which a contested logical principle is valid (to all those cases that are not deemed problematic); in all other cases they are fine in claiming that the principle is valid. Take, for example, the Logic of Paradox (LP) – roughly a kind of paraconsistent logic in which we have true contradictions but the consequence relation is not explosive (Priest 1979). In LP Priest observes that, in a semantically closed theory, using modus ponendo ponens (MPP) and absorption $(P\rightarrow(P\rightarrow Q))\vdash(P\rightarrow Q)$ a version of Curry's paradox is derivable.[100] In LP, $(A \rightarrow B)$ is defined as $(\neg A \vee B)$ (the material conditional), which suffices to establish that MPP can't in general be valid. For, if A is a dialetheia (a proposition both true and false), $(\neg A \vee B)$ is true even if B is not. MPP is labeled in LP as a quasi-valid rule, a rule that is valid provided that all truth-values involved are classical (i.e., solely true or solely false). Now, however, it appears that classical logic is more informative than LP. When asked, "Which instances of the contested principle hold?" classical logic responds: all, whereas non-classical logics (such as LP) respond: not all. Clearly, an "all" answer provides more information than a "not all" answer.

---

[98] We can naturally extend this characterization to a consequence relation $\vDash$: we say that a consequence relation $\vDash$ is stronger than another $\vDash*$ just in case whenever $\vDash*$ holds so does $\vDash$, but not vice versa. In a forthcoming paper titled "On Logical and Scientific Strength," Luca Incurvati and Carlo Nicolai (Incurvati & Nicolai 2024) develop an alternative understanding of logical strength in terms of interpretability strength, and they regard scientific strength as a special case of logical strength. The claimed advantage of their proposal is to offer a more flexible framework for understanding logical strength which promises to offer a unified approach to the comparison of formal theories.

[99] See Incurvati & Nicolai 2024 and Nicolai and Rossi 2018 for further discussion.

[100] Curry's paradox belongs to the family of so-called self-reference paradoxes (or paradoxes of circularity). Shortly, the paradox is derived in natural language from sentences like (a) "If sentence (a) is true, then Santa Claus exists." Suppose that the antecedent of the conditional in (a) is true, i.e. that sentence (a) is true. Then, by MPP Santa Claus exists. In this way the consequent of (a) is proved under the assumption of its antecedent. In other words, we have proved (a). Finally, by MPP, Santa Claus exists.

Such a lack of information may be mitigated by providing a principled reason for sharply individuating the class of statements for which the contested principle is taken to fail (e.g., a principled way of detecting vagueness in natural language expressions that would allow us to predict whether for a given statement S excluded middle would hold). However, even assuming that such a principled reason were available in all relevant cases, the resulting proposal would, firstly, complicate the theory, potentially adding ad hoc elements; and secondly, it would invariably depend on an extra-logical principle, necessitating further philosophical justification in the background, increasing thus the complexity of the theory.

After defining the concepts of logical and scientific strength as described, an interesting question emerges: how are the notions of logical and scientific strength related? Regarding this issue, there is considerable disagreement. Williamson claims that logical strength entails scientific strength for the reason that more deductive power yields more information. Moreover he believes that both logical and scientific strength are virtues. Russell (in Russell 2018) agrees with Williamson that scientific strength is a virtue but she rejects Williamson's claim that logical strength implies scientific strength and, moreover, she believes that logical strength should be considered neither a virtue nor a vice. In the model developed by Incurvati and Nicolai which employ translations between theories in accordance with suitable information-preserving constraints, we have that both scientific and logical strength are considered virtues.[101] Moreover, in their view, scientific strength entails logical strength but not vice versa, since not all translations involved in the relation of logical strength are adequate for scientific strength. Hjortland (in Hjortland 2017), adopts a more radical stance. He goes along with Williamson's characterization of logical strength but argues that logical weakness, and not logical strength, should be considered a virtue in a theory since it allows the theory to draw more, and more fine-grained, distinctions.

As evidenced by this short description of the current state of the art, there's ample disagreement on how to properly characterize the notion of strength as well as how to conceive of the relationship between logical and scientific strength. Although this disagreement is internal, as it were, to the abductivist camp, it nevertheless, and quite predictably, has significant consequences on the outcome of abductive comparison between rival logical theories.

As mentioned earlier, a second important element of theory comparison has to do with the comparative simplicity of rival theories. How should we

---

[101] Incurvati & Nicolai (2024).

understand simplicity?[102] Here the state of the debate within the philosophy of logic is less developed than in the case of the notion of strength. One intuitive way of characterizing simplicity is by means of avoidance of gerrymandered concepts or ad hoc hypotheses to account for phenomena that could be equally accounted for with more joint-carving concepts and avoiding the postulation of ad hoc hypotheses. Ceteris paribus, if two theories can equally explain a given set of phenomena but one theory, T1, uses more (or more gerrymandered) theoretical resources than the other theory T2, then T2 is favored over T1.[103] So for example, in science simple theories often have greater predictive power than more complex ones, making it easier to foresee outcomes and design experiments. Or, again, consider simplicity in its relation with the notion of elegance:[104] Scientists appreciate elegant theories that can explain a wide range of phenomena with minimal assumptions or complexity, rather than theories that are more complex and considered less elegant. Thus, a simpler theory can be chosen for pragmatic reasons (it is easier to handle) or for aesthetic reasons (it's more elegant). However, perhaps the most significant – and to some extent, controversial – reason for favouring a simpler theory concerns considerations regarding the relationship between simplicity and truth: ceteris paribus, a simpler theory is taken to be more plausible (more probable, or with a higher expected degree of predictive accuracy) than its less simple rivals.

The concept of simplicity poses notably intricate challenges in the philosophy of science, challenges that extend into the philosophy of logic as well. As Quine has pointed out, there may be a tension between simplifying the ontology and simplifying the ideology (as he calls it): roughly, postulating the existence of more entities may make the formulation of the theory simpler,[105] while simplifying the ideology making the formulation of the theory simpler, may require adding complexity to the ontology. And Ole Hjortland, writing about the issue of simplicity as a theoretical virtue in logic writes:

> A logic can be simple to use or simple to learn. It can be simple because it has few rules, or few models, because it has proofs of low complexity or models of low complexity. Some nonclassical logics have fewer rules than classical logic, but more models. Does that make them simpler or more complex?

---

[102] See Baker (2022) and Sober (2015) for a thorough discussion of the notion of simplicity.
[103] As Holsinger observes, cases where competing theories offer equally good explanations of a given phenomenon may be comparatively rare (Holsinger 1981).
[104] On the relationship between the theoretical virtue of simplicity and the aesthetic virtue of elegance, see Derkse (1992).
[105] Ontological simplicity can be qualitative, having to do with the number of kinds of things postulated, or merely quantitative, having to do with the number of individual things postulated. Arguably, Quine's point concerns qualitative simplicity.

> More models make it easier to refute an argument; more rules make it easier to prove a claim. (Hjortland 2017: 647)

Another interesting trade-off issue discussed by Elliot Sober concerns curve-fitting problems and can be put in terms of balancing simplicity (smoothing the curve and thus diminishing the risk of overfitting) and goodness-of-fit (accommodating all data points). As Sober asks: "If curve X is simpler than curve Y, but curve Y fits the data better than curve X, how are these two pieces of information to be combined into an overall judgment about the plausibility of the two curves?" (Sober 2002: 20).

This highlights the difficulties of providing an accurate measure of simplicity. However, a notion of simplicity is essential to explain what makes excessively complex hypotheses problematic, especially when they are on the verge of becoming ad hoc or gerrymandered. For this reason simplicity is widely taken to be a theoretical virtue that can be used effectively as a theory choice criterion both in science and logic.

5.2 Paradigmatic Examples of Logical Anti-Exceptionalism

In the rest of this section, we will swiftly explore some of the most prominent anti-exceptionalist viewpoints in the ongoing debate. The degree to which these diverse perspectives consider logic to be in continuity with the natural sciences depends on which of the various criteria mentioned earlier are taken on board. Our goal is not to offer an exhaustive overview of the perspectives of self-proclaimed anti-exceptionalists in logic. Many and variegated are in fact the views that have been proposed as a kind of logical anti-exceptionalism. Recent explorations into various forms of logical anti-exceptionalism, though not exhaustive, include: Newton Da Costa and Jonas Becker Arenhart,[106] Ole Hjortland,[107] Penelope Maddy,[108] Ben Martin,[109] Gillman Payette and Nicole Wyatt,[110] Jaroslav Peregrin and Vladimír Svoboda,[111] Graham Priest,[112] Stephen Read,[113] Gila Sher,[114] Gillian Russell,[115] Timothy Williamson.[116] Clearly this is not the venue for attempting a comprehensive review of all these works. Instead, we focus on examining key aspects of three paradigmatic

---

[106] Da Costa & Arenhart (2018).
[107] Hjortland (2017).
[108] Maddy (2022, Forthcoming).
[109] Martin (2021); Martin & Hjortland (2021)
[110] Payette & Wyatt (2018).
[111] Peregrin & Svoboda (2021).
[112] Priest (2005, 2014, 2016, 2019).
[113] Read (2019). Interestingly, Reads argues that while logic is methodologically unexceptional in being an a posteriori science, it is nevertheless analytic in the epistemic sense.
[114] Sher (2016, 2023, Forthcoming).
[115] Russell (2018, 2020).
[116] Williamson (2013, 2017, 2024, forthcoming_1).

anti-exceptionalist views – those of Timothy Williamson, Penelope Maddy, and the joint proposal by Ole Hjortland and Ben Martin – in order to better understand in what sense and to what extent they consider logic to be similar to the sciences.

Timothy Williamson, a staunch defender of classical logic, takes it as the abductively best logical theory in that it offers the best balance of the most important abductive values such as strength, simplicity, non-ad-hocness, and integration with scientific theories.[117] In recent works,[118] Williamson has argued that logic is not primarily about validity (or, more generally, about some kind of linguistic or metalinguistic entities), but it fundamentally concerns true law-like generalizations about the mostly non-linguistic world.[119] More specifically, Williamson takes the laws of (classical) logic, such as the law of excluded middle – which he formulates, allowing quantification in sentence position, as the universally quantified sentence $\forall P(P \vee \neg P)$ – to represent broad structural laws that govern the predominantly non-linguistic world. Essentially, he views them as fundamental principles underlying both logic and metaphysics. This conception of logical laws emphasizes that the true universal generalizations which correspond to logical truths are of primary importance. Their significance lies in the insights they provide about the world itself, rather than about the nature of logical truth or validity. In Williamson's view, then, our interest in these universal truths is not metalinguistic but as directly concerned with understanding reality as our engagement with the true statements of physics. In this respect Williamson's position strictly echoes Bertrand Russell's conception according to which "logic is concerned with the real world just as truly as zoology, though with its more abstract and general features" (Russell 1919: 169). It also shares with Gila Sher the idea that logical theories focus on the entities denoted by the logical constants, which include negation, conjunction, disjunction, identity, universal and other quantifiers, and possibly more, all of which play a role in nearly all forms of rigorous theoretical inquiry.[120] When expressed as universal generalizations, logical theorems do

---

[117] One of the chief ways of thinking of the background role of logic in the sciences is as a closure operator. We want to assess the hypotheses of our best scientific theories and we do that by inducing a mapping from each set of hypotheses H to its set of logical consequences CH according to our preferred logical system, where CH is the closure of H under its consequence relation. The closure relation satisfies all the classical structural rules, including, importantly, cut and contraction.

[118] See, specifically, Williamson (2017, 2018, forthcoming_1, 2024).

[119] Williamson is happy to concede that *superficially* the subject matter of logic concerns logical properties of sentences or propositions, such as logical truth and falsity, and logical relations between them, such as logical consequence and consistency. However, these linguistic objects and relations do not constitute logic's deep subject matter which is largely non-metalinguistic.

[120] See, especially, Sher (2016: 280–281).

not describe relationships between sentences but they articulate highly general patterns that pertain to the largely non-linguistic world.

Besides arguing for the theory of classical logic to be abductively the best logical theory in virtue of offering the best combination of strength and simplicity, Williamson's conception of logic fully qualifies as a science to a great extent, according to the criteria adopted here. Williamson sees logic as the most general science in that it involves generalizations that have a wider scope than those of any other science. Moreover, in concerning the mostly non-linguistic world the subject matter of logic is not of a kind totally dissimilar from the subject matter of the recognized sciences (paradigmatically, physics) and our methods for justifying or revising our logical theory are not dissimilar to those employed in justifying or revising our scientific theories.

Moreover, for Williamson logic plays some significant explanatory role. In its background role as an auxiliary formal tool for scientific theories, logic enhances the scientific strength of those theories as well as their explanatory and predictive power, by extracting more relevant consequences from them. Additionally, logic has an internal explanatory role in "subsuming isolated logical observations under illuminating generalizations – for example, in the twentieth-century streamlining of axioms for modal logic" (Williamson forthcoming 1).

Relatedly, Williamson takes our logical theory to be fundamentally descriptive of some of the most general aspects of the world. The laws of logic can be considered normative, but this is a derived sense of normativity tied to the undesirability (or impermissibility, according to the chosen normative principles) of holding (or inferring) false beliefs. This is exactly analogous to the normativity of physical laws: it is incorrect to maintain false beliefs about the physical world.

However, it must be stressed that Williamson's version of logical anti-exceptionalism is not a form of empiricism, since, contrary to what happens in the sciences, it gives no special role to experience to play. Indeed, logic, along with metaphysics and philosophy more broadly, is mostly conceived as an armchair pursuit. This divergence stems from the fact that in interpreted logic, unlike the natural sciences, evidence from experiment, observation, and measurement have usually no privileged role in accepting a theory. Moreover, despite accepting the general idea that logic is formal, he takes it not to offer a neutral tool for assessing competing metaphysical pictures. Taking logic to be such a neutral arbiter would mean to be forced to endorse some form of logical nihilism, which is certainly unwanted. This is because, simply, different philosophers have argued for different metaphysical views each of which puts into question one or more of the basic principles of classical logic. As a consequence, no single principle of classical logic has been immune from criticism on the basis of some metaphysical view.

All this being said, it is clear that for Williamson logic does not deviate from the standard process of theory formation and evaluation. Furthermore, experience is essential both for enabling beliefs in logical propositions and serving as evidence for/against them, in such a manner that neither aspect can be made null and void (contrary to what a sharp a-priori/a-posteriori distinction would demand). Although in Williamson's picture the role of empirical (dis)confirmation is significantly downplayed, without this meaning that logic does not concern reality, it is evident, from this brief discussion of his conception of logic, that Williamson provides an excellent example of a logical anti-exceptionalist who sees logic in significant continuity with the sciences in terms of methodology, epistemology, and metaphysics.

A different anti-exceptionalist stance for logic has been developed and defended by Penolepe Maddy in several of her works (e.g., Maddy 2007, 2014, forthcoming). Maddy advocates a naturalist and empiricist conception of logic – a conception that is the result of a more general viewpoint on philosophy that she calls *Second Philosophy*. A second philosopher is someone who is interested in all aspects of the world and our place in it. In Maddy's own words, such a philosopher, like a scientist

> [B]egins her investigation with every day perceptions, gradually develops more sophisticated approaches to observation and experimentation that expand her understanding and sometimes serve to correct her initial beliefs; eventually she begins to form and test hypotheses, and to engage in mature theory-formation and confirmation: along the way, she finds the need for, and pursue, first arithmetic and geometry, then analysis and even pure mathematics; and in all this, she often pauses to reflect on the methods she is using, to assess their effectiveness and improve them as she goes. (Maddy 2014, 93–94)

The second philosopher adopts the same attitude for all kinds of problems, including logical problems. Therefore, it's evident that Maddy perceives a substantial overlap between the methodologies and the epistemology of logic and the sciences. In this overlap, the role of empirical adequacy is relevant. To get an intuitive picture of what she is after, Maddy asks us to consider the following scenario: a subject S holds a concealed object in her hand, which could be either a common dime or an unfamiliar foreign coin (chosen randomly from a container with only these two types while blindfolded). Upon touching it, S discerns that it's not a dime, leading to the conclusion that it must be the foreign coin. The immediate question we may ask in relation to this scenario is the following: what does underlie this inference? When tackling such questions, the second philosopher approaches them as inquiries into the world. She begins by noting that the reliability of the coin inference and the truth of the corresponding conditional are not contingent on specific details about the physical composition or distinctive features of dimes. Instead, she asserts that only the following most general structural features of the situation really matter (which effectively exemplifies, at the objectual level, a reasoning pattern based on disjunctive syllogism): an object with one of two properties, lacking one, must possess the other. This insight is then systematically organized in the following way: For any object o and properties P and Q, if either o possesses P or o possesses Q and it is the case that o does not possess Q, then we conclude that o possesses P (and thus that the sentence "the object o possesses the property P" is true). Building on this foundation, the Second Philosopher develops a more comprehensive theory of forms that can generate widely applicable truths and reliable inferences. Maddy thus argues: "Suppose the Second Philosopher now codifies these features of her formal structures into a collection of inference patterns; coining a new term, she calls this 'rudimentary logic' [RL] (though without any preconceptions about the term 'logic'). She takes herself to have shown that this rudimentary logic is satisfied in any situation with formal structure" (Maddy 2014: 95).

Maddy contends that her conception of logic is influenced by the ideas of Kant and Wittgenstein who, she argues, take the validity of logical laws to stem from the structure of our physical world (Maddy 2007: 49). More specifically, Maddy's conception of what she calls "rudimentary logic" integrates two aspects: a transcendental one, of Kantian heritage, which positions logic at the core of our fundamental conceptualizations of the world; and an empirical one, according to which logic reveals the essential structure of the world. The aim of Maddy's approach is to have a comprehensive explanation that retains both features. For this purpose, Maddy characterizes an abstract Kant-Frege structure – the KF-world – encompassing objects, properties, and relations. In contrast to conventional first-order structures, KF-worlds incorporate ground-consequent dependencies and uncertainties, giving rise to a rudimentary logic, RL. RL describes the macroworld, supported by common sense and science. Human beings accept it due to innate cognitive mechanisms recognizing the world's KF-structure.[121] Moreover, human cognitive structures align with RL because the macroworld follows a KF-world pattern. As evident from this brief description, Maddy's position in the philosophy of logic sees logic and the sciences to be aligned in both methodological and epistemological terms.

---

[121] Maddy draws on 1990s infant cognition studies to show humans can grasp KF-structures early, without language or extensive experience. Our cognition naturally leans toward accepting basic RL inferences.

Differently from Williamson, Maddy fully embraces a naturalistic perspective that assigns to experience and empirical adequacy a more prominent role.

As a third example of an anti-exceptionalist conception of logic, let us consider the most recent proposal by Ole Hjortland and Ben Martin, which they label "logical predictivism." Logical predictivism is grounded in two, arguably uncontroversial, facts: (a) scientific theories strive to explain specific phenomena, and (b) scientific theories demonstrate their efficacy, at least in part, by generating accurate predictions. According to logical predictivism, we should take logical theories to be analogous to scientific theories in these crucial respects. In other words, logical theories should be, at least partially, evaluated on their ability to explain a given set of target phenomena and to make successful predictions. In their own words: "Logics then have phenomena they attempt to explain, and use successful predictions as a criterion to judge the fruitfulness of these explanations. [...] [I]f our predictivist account is ultimately successful in reflecting how logicians go about supporting their theories, this will go a considerable way to substantiating the methodological anti-exceptionalist's claims" (Martin & Hjortland 2021: 288).

Hjortland and Martin argue that to provide meaningful insights into a target phenomenon and formulate predictions that are amenable to empirical testing, it is crucial to depart from the conventional idea that logical theories are just a set of valid inference rules or theorems. Instead, they propose to consider logical theories as comprehensive frameworks having as essential components definitions (e.g., let $\neg\varphi$ be Boolean negation), laws (e.g.: For every valuation, all sentences are either true or false, and not both), and representation rules (such as: $\ulcorner not\ \varphi \urcorner = \ulcorner \neg\varphi \urcorner$, or $\ulcorner if\ \varphi\ then\ \psi \urcorner = \ulcorner \varphi \rightarrow \psi \urcorner$). All the aforementioned elements not only provide the underlying semantics but also contribute to the syntax of the theory, laying the groundwork for a formalization of natural language expressions.

Moreover, within the predictivist framework – which sees with a friendly eye a practice-based approach to the epistemology of logic – theories find their initial motivation in instances of arguments which are assessed as acceptable by reliable practitioners. This frequently involves informal mathematical proofs, which are assessed as acceptable by mathematicians, or alternatively, natural-language arguments assessed as acceptable by reliable reasoners (Martin and Hjortland: forthcoming). Consider the case of mathematical proofs. In such cases the mathematicians' assessments of acceptable inferences serve as a reliable (but of course fallible) guide to distinguishing valid from invalid proofs. It is the task of the logician to argue why certain proofs are held valid or invalid. To do this, a logician follows a number of steps. First, she conjectures that inferences across multiple proofs may be (in)valid for similar reasons, sharing some underlying structure. Secondly, she puts forth a specific hypothesis regarding the validity of an argument form observed in "acceptable" informal proofs. This hypothesis, on its own, does not function as an explanation for the validity of the target proofs; it merely represents a generalization that can later be subject to additional confirmation or falsification. They argue that

> [I]n order to explain why arguments of this form are valid (if they are), our logician must propose a theory [...] that provides a set of postulates prescribing the behavior of the argument's components and the consequence relation. The aim is for this theory to be able to explain why the given hypothesis is true [...], by showing that the arguments' validity results from the theories' definitions and laws. (Martin & Hjortland forthcoming-b: 7)

They propose to consider an adequate explanation, something entailing a detailed description on how the inherent structure of these arguments guarantees their validity. Subsequently, such a theory should be tested to understand if it is preferable to competing theories. A method of accomplishing this is by generating predictions based on the theory's postulates and then validating these predictions through testing. A way of testing them is to ask the relevant group of subjects, for instance mathematicians, whether they consider the target inferences acceptable or not. The assumption is that mathematicians' judgments on the acceptability of proofs can be considered as a guide to the validity of the inferences at issue. The logician assesses the theory's support based on how well mathematicians' judgments align with the theory's predictions. If there is agreement between judgments and predictions, the theory gains further support; conversely, if discrepancies arise, the theory encounters challenges that must be addressed or reconciled, analogously to what happens in the natural sciences. Unlike Williamson and Maddy's approach, Martin and Hjortland's logical predictivism focuses on validity as the primary concern of logical theories. They consider the most relevant data for assessing a theory's adequacy to be considered judgments about instances of logical rules of inference. Their testing methodology is in line with standard methodology within the practice-based philosophies of science and mathematics.

Conclusions

In this Element, our primary goal has been to offer a detailed and systematic exploration of the intricate relationship between logic and science, going beyond what recent literature in the philosophy of logic, especially that on logical anti-exceptionalism, provides. We hope that this contributes to enhancing our understanding of one of the most debated topics in recent trends in the philosophy of logic, specifically logical anti-exceptionalism.

Undoubtedly, logical anti-exceptionalism, as a broad perspective on the discipline of logic, possesses considerable merits. One notable virtue, as evident from the three examples discussed in Section 5.2, is that it offers an insightful and systematic discussion of the methodological aspects of logic. Furthermore, by viewing logic as being in broad continuity with the sciences, logical anti-exceptionalism presents an epistemology of logic and of our inferential practices that aligns closely with those found in the sciences and in scientific practices. The advantage of this approach is, arguably, that of avoiding the need for postulating ad hoc mental attitudes (such as rational insights and similar attitudes) or seemingly recherché justificatory strategy, thereby seamlessly integrating logic as a discipline into the wider body of our scientific knowledge and practices.

Despite its merits, logical anti-exceptionalism remains a controversial stance concerning the philosophy of logic, with important limitations and unresolved issues. We won't have the opportunity to delve into the various criticisms leveled against logical anti-exceptionalism, and more broadly, against the thesis that there is significant continuity between logic and science. However, let's briefly touch upon a few broad issues that are currently debated. These issues relate to three key areas where logical anti-exceptionalists have made distinctive claims, namely on the metaphysics, the methodology, and the epistemology of logic.

Let's start with the metaphysics first. One very broad issue concerns the fact that various proposals within the logical anti-exceptionalist camp rely, to a variable degree, on a naturalistic and realist conception of logic. These are not free of objections. Take a realistic conception of logic. One of the core tenets of logical realism is the thesis that logical relations and logical facts exist somewhat independently of the mind and language. The precise nature of these facts and relations differs depending on the specific view. A first and quite straightforward consequence of realism is a lack of impartiality about what metaphysical stance on reality to adopt. In this respect, such a conception challenges the idea of the neutrality of logic, as it was traditionally conceived. Indeed, contrary to being detached from the nature of reality, in this perspective logic appears intimately linked to reality (perhaps, to certain of its structural features). Thus, within a realist conception of the nature of logic, distinguishing between metaphysics and logic becomes rather challenging. As Williamson noted, the fact that logic is not indifferent with respect to what reality is like can be displayed by logical rivalries resulting from metaphysical considerations: "For example, rejection of the law of excluded middle has been based on metaphysical conceptions of the future or of infinity. Quantum mechanics has been interpreted as showing the invalidity of one of the distributive laws. Dialetheists believe that paradoxes about sets or change manifest black holes of contradiction in reality itself" (Williamson 2014).

If this is the case, and logic reflects worldly structures, thereby playing a role in determining the correct metaphysical view, its logical truths carry metaphysical commitments. Now, given the proliferation of logical systems and logical theories one may sensibly ask, within a broadly realistic conception of logic, whether they are all in the business of describing the same reality? And if yes, how do we adjudicate between rival logics? Moreover, if logical realism is combined with logical pluralism – the idea that there's more than one correct logic[122] – what are the metaphysical consequences of this combination? In particular, is the derived picture a form of metaphysical pluralism? Alternatively, does a variety of non-neutral logics collectively contribute to defining a singular set of metaphysical truths?

Consider, then, a broadly Quinean naturalistic conception of logic. As seen before, Quine argues for a naturalistic stance in logic: the justification of logical laws parallels the methods used for justifying non-logical laws. It is done not in isolation but as an integral part of overall theory-choice, substantiated by similar types of evidence. Such a conception in logic is aligned in Quine with his conception of logic: "it is within science itself, and not in some prior philosophy, that reality is to be identified and described" (1981: 21). The implication is that our best scientific theory provides us as much as we know about reality.

However, Martin and Hjortland observe that "it would be a mistake [...] to conclude that in general contemporary anti-exceptionalists are naturalists" (Martin and Hjortland, *forthcoming*). One paradigmatic example of a naturalistic anti-exceptionalism is Maddy's Second Philosophy. A second philosopher is one who argues that logical truths are the most general truths about the world pertaining to the structural features of the world, the KF-structures, giving rise to what Maddy calls a rudimentary logic. Such a philosopher starts her inquiry by delving into commonplace perceptions, progressively refining her methods of observation and experimentation to enhance comprehension and occasionally rectify initial beliefs. When and why is a naturalist conception in logic coupled with a metaphysical naturalism? What are pros and cons of such a metaphysical conception of logic?

---

[122] On logical pluralism see, for instance, Beall & Restall (2006), Shapiro (2014), Eklund (2020), Russell & Blake-Turner (2023), and Caret (forthcoming).

Let us now briefly discuss a couple of significant challenges that target methodological and epistemological aspects of logical anti-exceptionalist views. Different philosophers, starting from different background theoretical assumptions, but using the same broad abductive methodology for theory choice have reached quite different conclusions concerning which is the correct all-purpose logic. Williamson (2017) advocates classical logic; Priest (2016) advocates the paraconsistent logic LP; Hjortland (2017) and Russell (Blake-Turner & Russell 2018) advocate logical pluralism. Why is it that, despite employing a similar overarching methodology and considering the same abductively relevant criteria (strength, simplicity, avoidance of ad hoc stipulations, etc.), different philosophers have identified various winners in the abductive competition? As Ulf Hlobil points out: "[B]efore we can apply an abductive methodology, we must settle on points that are not neutral with respect to many foundational disputes. As a result, abductivism cannot provide a neutral method for choosing a logic" (Hlobil 2021: 323).

One of these points which are not neutral with respect to foundational disputes has to do with the nature of the relevant data that the competing theories are expected to account for. As Hlobil argues, different logical theories have different views about which are the relevant data. Under the assumption that rival logical theories are competing over which logic is the correct logic of reality there won't be any agreement on which is the data to be explained. From a broadly epistemicist conception it may be argued that this is just a (perhaps not so uncommon) epistemological impasse which should not be taken to suggest that there's no fact of the matter of which is the correct logic (and which are the relevant data to be explained). However, this kind of reaction may be seen as particularly unappealing in the case at issue since it is not at all clear what is exactly that the advocates of the various rival logics would be ignorant about. They start from different theoretical assumptions and they would consider different sets of data as being relevant for justifying their preferred logic. Since it is a rather controversial matter what the relevant data are in the case of logic, there's not even a settled target phenomenon about which all disputants may agree that there's something we are ignorant about. And it seems also clear that we cannot resolve this meta-dispute by pointing to some additional data. This general issue constitutes a significant limitation of the kind of abductivism that is at the core of many anti-exceptionalist methodologies.

On the epistemological side, arguably, one of the most challenging objections to logical anti-exceptionalism of Quinean lineage has been mounted by Crispin Wright (especially in Wright 1986 and revisited in Wright 2021).[123] As we have

---

[123] Stewart Shapiro (in Shapiro 2000) and Ben Martin (in Martin 2021) discuss a somewhat related issue that Martin calls "the background logic problem."

seen in Section 2, one of the core tenets of Quine's epistemology is that nothing is in principle immune to revision on the basis of empirical evidence – not even core logical principles. When a situation of recalcitrance happens such that a certain observation O (which is taken by a theory T to be a consequence of a set of initial conditions I) is found to be incorrect (because as a matter of fact our evidence E in incompatible with O), everything that is involved in reaching the acknowledgment of such a situation of recalcitrance is open to revision. This includes the theory T, the claim that E agrees with I but disagrees with O, the epistemic good standing of E, the logic L that allows us to derive within T the testing conditional, as Wright calls it, that I implies O (I→O), and, crucially, the claim that such a conditional is indeed an L-consequence of T – that is, a statement that is derivable from T by some rule R of L. Wright's objection, to put it concisely, is that it is incoherent to maintain that situations of recalcitrance as those just illustrated allow us to hold accountable not just the empirical premises of the scientific theory but also any aspect of the logico-inferential apparatus involved, in particular the good standing of the rule R which allowed us to derive the testing conditional from T. In order to even appreciate that there is a problem (a situation of recalcitrance) in the first place, we need to presuppose the epistemic good standing of R. As Wright puts the point:

> There is incoherence in the idea that the case for revising a rule of inference, R, might rest on a derivation of a Problem – a situation of "recalcitrance" – in circumstances where the derivation relies essentially on R itself. The key thought is that the belief that you really have a Problem, which rationality requires you to remedy, must rely on the belief that your derivation is sound, so on a belief that R is good. If you then query that, you undermine your reason for thinking that you have a Problem in the first place. (Wright 2021: 341)

Thus, even conceding that logic is by and large unexceptional, we must take some of its most basic principles (e.g., modus ponens and universal instantiation) as being by default in epistemic good standing and thus removed from the dynamics of any process of empirical theory testing.

While none of these objections are definitive on their own, collectively they pose a significant and intriguing set of challenges. Any theory of logic that seeks to bridge logic and science must thoughtfully engage with these challenges, inviting a deeper exploration into the intricate relationship between logic and science.

References

Agassi, J. (1991). Popper's Demarcation of Science Refuted. Methodology and Science, 24: 1–7.

Anderson, A. R., & Belnap, N. D. (1975). Entailment: The Logic of Relevance and Necessity. Princeton: Princeton University Press.

Ayer, A. J. (1936). Language, Truth and Logic. Mineola: Dover.

Baker, A. (2022). Simplicity. Stanford Encyclopaedia of Philosophy. https://plato.stanford.edu/archives/sum2022/entries/simplicity/.

Beall, J. C., & Restall, G. (2006). Logical Pluralism. New York: Oxford University Press.

Bennett, J. (2003). A Philosophical Guide to Conditionals. Oxford: Clarendon Press.

Blake-Turner, C., & Russell, G. (2018). Logical Pluralism without the Normativity. Synthese, 198: 4859–4877.

Blancke, S., & Boudry, M. (2021). Pseudoscience as a Negative Outcome of Scientific Dialogue: A Pragmatic-Naturalistic Approach to the Demarcation Problem. International Studies in the Philosophy of Science, 34(3), 183–198, https://doi.org/10.1080/02698595.2022.2057777.

Blancke, S., Boudry, M., & Pigliucci, M. (2017). Why Do Irrational Beliefs Mimic Science? The Cultural Evolution of Pseudoscience. Theoria, 83(1): 78–97. https://doi.org/10.1111/theo.12109.

Bobzien, S. (2020). Ancient Logic. The Stanford Encyclopedia of Philosophy (Summer Edition), Edward N. Zalta (Ed.), https://plato.stanford.edu/archives/sum2020/entries/logic-ancient/.

Boghossian, P. (1996). Analyticity Reconsidered. Noûs, 30, 360–391.

Boghossian, P. A. (2003). Epistemic Analyticity: A Defense. Grazer Philosophische Studien, 66(1): 15–35.

Boghossian, P., & Williamson, T. (2020). Debating the a priori. Oxford: Oxford University Press.

Boghossian, P., & Wright, C. (2023). Kripke, Quine, the "Adoption Problem," and the Empirical Conception of Logic. Mind, 133(529): 86–116.

Bonnay, D. (2014). Logical Constants, or How to Use Invariance in Order to Complete the Explication of Logical Consequence. Philosophy Compass, 9(1): 54–65.

Bonnay, D., & Speitel, S. G. W. (2021). The Ways of Logicality: Invariance and Categoricity. In G. Sagi & J. Woods (Eds.), The Semantic Conception of

Logic: Essays on Consequence, Invariance, and Meaning. New York: Cambridge University Press, pp. 55–79.

Boudry, M. (2017). Plus Ultra: Why Science Does Not Have Limits. In M. Boudry & M. Pigliucci (Eds.), Science Unlimited? The Challenges of Scientism. Chicago: University of Chicago Press, pp. 31–52.

Boudry, M. (2022). Diagnosing Pseudoscience – by Getting Rid of the Demarcation Problem. Journal for General Philosophy of Science, 83–101. https://doi.org/10.1007/s10838-021-09572-4.

Brandom, R. (2018). From Logical Expressivism to Expressivist Logic: Sketch of a Program and Some Implementations. Philosophical Issues, 28(1), 70–88.

Bunge, M. (1984). What Is Pseudoscience? The Skeptical Inquirer, 9(1): 36–47.

Burge, T. (2003). Logic and Analyticity. Grazer Philosophische Studien, 66: 199–249.

Burgess, J. P. (2014). Quine's Philosophy of Logic and Mathematics. In G. Harman & E. Lepore (Eds.), A Companion to W. V. O. Quine. Oxford: Wiley, pp. 279–295.

Caret, C. (forthcoming). Logical Pluralism. Cambridge: Cambridge University Press.

Carnap, R. (1959). The Elimination of Metaphysics through Logical Analysis of Language. In A. J. Ayer (Ed.), Logical Positivism. New York: The Free Press, pp. 60–81.

Commandeur, L. (2023). Logical Instrumentalism and Anti-exceptionalism about Logic. *Erkenntnis*, 1–21.

Cook, R. (2000). Logic-as-Modelling: A New Perspective on Formalization. PhD Dissertation, The Ohio State University, Columbus.

Cook, R. (2010). Let a Thousand Flowers Bloom: A Tour of Logical Pluralism. Philosophy Compass, 5(6): 492–504.

Cook, R. (forthcoming). Logic-as-Modelling. In F. Ferrari, E. Brendel, M. Carrara, et al. (Eds.), The Oxford Handbook of Philosophy of Logic. Oxford: Oxford University Press.

Da Costa, N., & Arenhart, J. (2018). Full-blooded Anti-exceptionalism. Australasian Journal of Logic, 15(2): 362–380.

Dawes, G. W. (2018). Identifying Pseudoscience: A Social Process Criterion. Journal for General Philosophy of Science, 49(3): 283–298. https://doi.org/10.1007/s10838-017-9388-6.

De Morgan, A. (1858). On the Syllogism: III. Transactions of the Cambridge Philosophical Society 10, 173–230. Reprinted in De Morgan 1966, 74–146.

De Morgan, A. (1966). On the Syllogism (and Other Logical Writings). Ed. Peter Heath. New Haven: Yale University Press.

References

Derkse, W. (1992). On Simplicity and Elegance. Delft: Eburon.

Dummett, M. (1973). Frege: Philosophy of Language. London: Duckworth.

Dummett, M. (1976). Is Logic Empirical?, in H. D. Lewis (Ed.), Contemporary British Philosophy, 4th series. London: Allen and Unwin, pp. 45–68.

Dummett, M. (1991). The Logical Basis of Metaphysics. Cambridge: Harvard University Press.

Dunn, J. M., & Restall, G. (2002). Relevance Logic. In D. Gabbay & F. Guenthner (Eds.), Handbook of Philosophical Logic (2nd ed., Vol. 6, pp. 1–128). Berlin: Springer.

Dutilh Novaes, C. (2014). The Undergeneration of Permutation Invariance as a Criterion for Logicality. Erkenntnis, 79(1): 81–97.

Eklund, M. (2020). Making Sense of Logical Pluralism. Inquiry, 63(3–4): 433–454.

Elgin, C. Z., & Adler, J. E. (1980). Reviewed Work(s): Philosophical Papers by Imre Lakatos, John Worrall and Gregory Currie. Synthese, 43(3): 411–420.

Etchemendy, J. (1990). The Concept of Logical Consequence. Cambridge: Harvard University Press.

Feferman, S. (1999). Logic, Logics, and Logicism. Notre Dame Journal of Formal Logic, 40(1): 31–54.

Feferman, S. (2010). Set-theoretical Invariance Criteria for Logicality. Notre Dame Journal of Formal Logic, 51(1): 3–20.

Ferrari, F. (2022). Truth and Norms. London: Lexington.

Ferrari, F., & Hlobil, U. (forthcoming). The Normativity of Logic. In F. Ferrari et al. (Eds.), The Oxford Handbook of Philosophy of Logic. Oxford: Oxford University Press.

Field, H. (1996). The Apriority of Logic. Proceedings of the Aristotelian Society, 96: 359–379.

Fine, K. (2002). The Varieties of Necessity. In J. Hawthorne & T. S. Gendler (Eds.), Conceivability and Possibility. Oxford: Oxford University Press, pp. 253–282.

Frege, G. (1893–1903). Grundgesetze der Arithmetik, begriffsschriftlich abgeleitet. Two volumes. Jena: Pohle. Partial translation in Frege 1964.

Frege, G. (1918). Der Gedanke. Eine Logische Untersuchung, Beiträge zur Philosophie des deutschen Idealismus, I (1918–1919): 58–77; Translated as 'Thoughts', by P. Geach and R. Stoothoff, in McGuinness (Ed.) 1984, pp. 351–372.

Frege, G. (1953). The Foundations of Arithmetic: A Logico-Mathematical Enquiry into the Concept of Number. Oxford: Blackwell. Translation by J. L. Austin of Frege, G. (1884). Die Grundlagen der Arithmetik: eine logisch mathematische Untersuchung über den Begriff der Zahl. Breslau: Willhelm Koebner.

Frege, G. (1964). The Basic Laws of Arithmetic: Exposition of the System. Trans. M. Furth. Berkeley: University of California Press.

Frege, G. (1967). Begriffsschrift. In J. van Heijenoort (Ed.), From Frege to Gödel. Cambridge: Harvard University Press, pp. 5–82.

Frege, G. (1979). Posthumous Writings. Ed. by Peter Long and Roger White. Chicago: University of Chicago Press.

Glanzberg, M. (2021). Models, Model Theory, and Modeling. In G. Sagi & J. Woods (Eds.), The Semantic Conception of Logic. Cambridge: Cambridge University Press, pp. 209–226.

Griffiths, O., & Paseau, A. (forthcoming). Formal Validity: Model-Theoretic and Proof-Theoretic Conceptions. In F. Ferrari, E. Brendel, M. Carrara, et al. (Eds.), The Oxford Handbook of Philosophy of Logic. Oxford: Oxford University Press.

Haack, S. (1974). Deviant Logic: Some Philosophical Issues. Cambridge: Cambridge University Press.

Haack, S. (1975). Quine's Theory of Logic. Erkenntnis, 13(2): 231–259.

Haack, S. (1978). Philosophy of Logics. Cambridge: Cambridge University Press.

Hanna, R. (2009). Rationality and Logic. Cambridge: The MIT Press.

Hansson, S. O. (2006). Falsificationism Falsified. Foundations of Science, 11: 275–286.

Hansson, S. O. (2013). Defining Pseudoscience and Science. In M. Pigliucci & M. Boudry (Eds.), Philosophy of Pseudoscience: Reconsidering the Demarcation Problem. Chicago: Chicago University Press, pp. 61–77.

Hansson, S. O. (2020). Disciplines, Doctrines, and Deviant Science. International Studies in the Philosophy of Science, 33(1): 43–52. https://doi.org/10.1080/02698595.2020.1831258.

Hansson, S. O. (2021). Science and Pseudo-Science. In E. N. Zalta (Ed.), The Stanford Encyclopedia of Philosophy (Fall Ed.). https://plato.stanford.edu/archives/fall2021/entries/pseudo-science/.

Hempel, C. G. (1951). The Concept of Cognitive Significance: A Reconsideration. Proceedings of the American Academy of Arts and Sciences, 80, 61–77.

Hirvonen, I., & Karisto, J. (2022). Demarcation without Dogmas. Theoria, 88: 701–720.

Hjortland, O. (2017). Anti-exceptionalism about Logic. Philosophical Studies, 174(3): 631–658.

Hlobil, U. (2021). Limits of Abductivism about Logic. Philosophy and Phenomenological Research, 103(2): 320–340.

Hofweber, T. (2021). The Unrevisability of Logic. Philosophical Perspectives, 35: 251–274.

Holman, B., & Wilholt, T. (2022). The New Demarcation Problem. Studies in History and Philosophy of Science, 91: 211–220. https://doi.org/10.1016/j.shpsa.2021.11.011.

Holsinger, K. (1981). Comment: The Blunting of Occam's Razor, or to Hell with Parsimony. Canadian Journal of Zoology, 59(1): 144–146.

Horwich, P. (1998). Truth (2nd ed.). New York: Oxford University Press.

Hylton, P. (2007). Quine. Milton Park, Abingdon-on-Thames: Routledge.

Incurvati, L., & Nicolai, C. (2024). On Logical and Scientific Strength. Erkenntnis, https://doi.org/10.1007/s10670-024-00835-2.

Kahneman, D. (2011). Thinking Fast and Slow. New York: Farrar, Straus & Giroux.

Kant, I. (1929). Critique of Pure Reason. New York: Macmillan.

Keas, M. N. (2017). Systematizing the Theoretical Virtues. Synthese, 195: 2761–2793.

Klein, F. (1872). Vergleichende Betrachtungen über neuere geometrische Forschungen. Andreas Deichert.

Kreisel, G. (1971). A Survey of Proof Theory II, in J. E. Fenstad (Ed.), Proceedings of the Second Scandinavian Logic Symposium, vol. 63 of Studies in Logic and the Foundations of Mathematics, North-Holland, Amsterdam, 1971, pp. 109–170.

Kripke, S. (2023). The Question of Logic. Mind, 133 (529): 1–36.

Kuhn, T. S. (1977). Objectivity, Value Judgment, and Theory Choice. In The Essential Tension: Selected Studies in Scientific Tradition and Change. Chicago: University of Chicago Press, pp. 320–339.

Ladyman, J., & Ross, D. (2007). Every Thing Must Go: Metaphysics Naturalized. Oxford: Oxford University Press.

Lakatos, I. (1978). The Methodology of Scientific Research Programmes. Cambridge: Cambridge University Press.

Laudan, L. (1983). The Demise of the Demarcation Problem. In R. S. Cohen & L. Laudan (Eds.), Physics, Philosophy and Psychoanalysis. Boston Studies in the Philosophy of Science, (Vol. 76). Dordrecht: Springer, pp. 111–127.

Leech, J. (2015). Logic and the Laws of Thought. Philosophers' Imprint, 15: 1–27.

Leitgeb, H. (2023). Vindicating the Verifiability Criterion. Philosophical Studies (online first: https://doi.org/10.1007/s11098-023-02071-w).

Letrud, K. (2019). The Gordian Knot of Demarcation: Tying Up Some Loose Ends. International Studies in the Philosophy of Science, 32(1): 3–11. https://doi.org/10.1080/02698595.2019.1618031.

Lipton, P. (2004). Inference to the Best Explanation. London: Routledge & Taylor and Francis.

Lutz, S. (2011). On an Allegedly Essential Feature of Criteria for the Demarcation of Science. The Reasoner, 5(8): 125–126.

MacFarlane, J. (2000). What Does It Mean to Say That Logic Is Formal? [PhD Thesis, University of Pittsburgh].

MacFarlane, J. (2002). Frege, Kant, and the Logic in Logicism. The Philosophical Review, 111: 25–65.

MacFarlane, J. (2004). In What Sense (if any) Is Logic Normative? Published in Russian with the title "В каком смысле, если он вообще есть, логика нормативна по отношению к мышлению?". In Современная логика: Основания, предмет и перспективы развития [Modern Logic: Its Subject Matter, Foundations and Prospects], ed. Д.В. Зайцева [D. Zaitsev] (Москва [Moscow]: ИД Форум [Forum], 2018).

MacFarlane, J., "Logical Constants", The Stanford Encyclopedia of Philosophy (Winter 2017 Edition), E. N. Zalta (Ed.), https://plato.stanford.edu/archives/win2017/entries/logical-constants/.

Maddy, P. (2007). Second Philosophy: A Naturalistic Method. Oxford: Oxford University Press.

Maddy, P. (2012). The Philosophy of Logic. Bulletin of Symbolic Logic, 18(4), 481–504.

Maddy, P. (2014). The Logical Must. New York: Oxford University Press.

Maddy, P. (2022). A Plea for Natural Philosophy and Other Essays. New York: Oxford University Press.

Maddy, P. (forthcoming). Varieties of Naturalism in Logic. In F. Ferrari, E. Brendel, M. Carrara, et al. (Eds.), The Oxford Handbook of Philosophy of Logic. Oxford University Press.

Mahner, M. (2013). Science and Pseudoscience: How to Demarcate after the (Alleged) Demise of the Demarcation Problem. In M. Pigliucci & M. Boudry (Eds.), pp. 29–43.

Martin, B. (2021). Anti-Exceptionalism about Logic and the Burden of Explanation. Canadian Journal of Philosophy, 51(8): 602–618.

Martin, B., & Hjortland, O. (2021). Logical Predictivism. Journal of Philosophical Logic, 50: 285–318.

Martin, B., & Hjortland, O. (2022). Anti-Exceptionalism about Logic as Tradition Rejection. Synthese, 200(148). https://doi.org/10.1007/s11229-022-03653-7.

References

Martin, B., & Hjortland, O. (2024). Evidence in Logic. In M. Lasonen-Aarnio & C. M. Littlejohn (Eds.), Routledge Handbook of the Philosophy of Evidence. Routledge.

Martin, B., & Hjortland, O. (forthcoming). Anti-Exceptionalism about Logic II: Methodological Anti-Exceptionalism about Logic. Forthcoming in *Philosophy Compass*.

McGee, V. (1996). Logical Operations. Journal of Philosophical Logic, 25: 567–580.

McIntyre, L. (2019). The Scientific Attitude. Defending Science Form Denial, Fraud, and Pseudoscience. Cambridge: MIT Press.

Mezzadri, D. (2015a). Frege on the Normativity and Constitutivity of Logic for Thought I. Philosophy Compass, 10(9): 583–591.

Mezzadri, D. (2015b). Frege on the Normativity and Constitutivity of Logic for Thought II. Philosophy Compass, 10(9): 592–600.

Milne, P. (1994). Classical Harmony: Rules of Inference and the Meaning of the Logical Constants. Synthese, 100: 49–94.

Newton-Smith, W. (1981). The Rationality of Science. Boston: Routledge.

Nicolai, C., & Rossi, L. (2018). Principles for Object-Linguistic Consequence: From Logical to Irreflexive. Journal of Philosophical Logic, 47(3): 549–577.

Oza, M. (2020). The Value of Thinking and the Normativity of Logic. Philosophers' Imprint, 20(25): 1–23.

Paseau, A. C., & Griffiths, O. (2022). One True Logic: A Monist Manifesto. Oxford: Oxford University Press.

Payette, G., & Wyatt, N. (2018). Logical Particularism. In J. Wyatt, N. J.L. L. Pedersen & N. Kellen (Eds.), Pluralisms in Truth and Logic. New York: Palgrave. pp. 277–299.

Peregrin, J., & Svoboda, V. (2021). Moderate Anti-exceptionalism and Earthborn Logic. Synthese, 199(3–4): 8781–8806.

Pigliucci, M., & Boudry, M. (Eds.) (2013). Philosophy of Pseudoscience: Reconsidering the Demarcation Problem. Chicago: Chicago University Press.

Popper, K. (1962). Conjectures and Refutations: The Growth of Scientific Knowledge. New York: Basic Books.

Popper, K. [1989] 1994. Falsifizierbarkeit, zwei Bedeutungen von. In H. Seiffert & G. Radnitzky, Handlexikon zur Wissenschaftstheorie, 2nd ed., München: Ehrenwirth GmbH Verlag, pp. 82–86.

Priest, G. (1979). The Logic of Paradox. Journal of Philosophical Logic, 8(1): 219–241.

Priest, G. (2006). Doubt Truth to be a Liar. Oxford: Oxford University Press.

Priest, G. (2014). Revising Logic. ch. 12 of P. Rush (Ed.), The Metaphysics of Logic, Cambridge: Cambridge University Press.

Priest, G. (2016). Logical Disputes and the a Priori. Logique et Analyse, 236: 347–66.

Priest, G. (2019). Logical Theory-Choice: The Case of Vacuous Counterfactuals. Australasian Journal of Logic, 16(7): 283–297.

Prior, A. (1960). A Runabout Inference Ticket. Analysis, 21(2): 38–39.

Putnam, H. (1968). Is Logic Empirical? In R. S. Cohen & M. W. Wartofsky (Eds.), Boston Studies in the Philosophy of Science (Vol. 5). Dordrecht: Springer, pp. 216–241.

Putnam, H. (2005). A Philosopher Looks at Quantum Mechanics (again). British Journal for the Philosophy of Science, 56: 615–634.

Quine, W. V. O. (1936). Truth by Convention. In A. N. Whitehead (Ed.), Philosophical Essays for Alfred North Whitehead. New York: Longmans, Green, pp. 90–124.

Quine, W. V. O. (1948). On What There Is. The Review of Metaphysics, 2(5): 21–38.

Quine, W. V. O. (1951). Main Trends in Recent Philosophy: Two Dogmas of Empiricism. The Philosophical Review, 60(1): 20–43. https://doi.org/10.2307/2181906.

Quine, W. V. O (1956). Quantifiers and Propositional Attitudes. The Journal of Philosophy, 53(5): 177–187.

Quine, W. V. O. (1963). Carnap and Logical Truth. In P. A. Schilpp (Ed.), The Philosophy of Rudolf Carnap. LaSalle: Open Court, pp. 385–406.

Quine, W. V. O. (1975a). Carnap and Logical Truth. In W.V.O. Quine (Ed.), The Ways of Paradox and Other Essays. Cambridge: Harvard University Press, pp. 107–132.

Quine, W. V. O. (1975b). Theories and Things. Cambridge, MA: Harvard University Press, 1981.

Quine, W. V. O. (1981) Theories and Things. Cambridge, MA: Harvard University Press.

Quine, W. V. (1986a). Philosophy of Logic (2nd ed.). Cambridge: Harvard University Press.

Quine, W. V. (1986b). Reply to Geoffrey Hellman. In L. E. Hahn & P. A. Schilpp (Eds.), The Philosophy of W. V. Quine. London: Open Court, pp. 206–208.

Quine, W. V. (1986c). Reply to Jules Vuillemin. In L. E. Hahn & P. A. Schilpp (Eds.), The Philosophy of W. V. Quine. London: Open Court, pp. 279–295.

Quine, W. V. (1986d). Reply to Charles Parsons. In L. E. Hahn & P. A. Schilpp (Eds.), The Philosophy of W. V. Quine. London: Open Court, pp. 396–403.

Quine, W. V. O. (1990). Pursuit of Truth, Cambridge, MA: Harvard University Press.

Quine, W. V. O. (1995). From Stimulus to Science. Cambridge: Harvard University Press.

Radner, D., & Radner, M. (1982). Science and Unreason. Belmont: Wadsworth.

Rayo, A. (Ed.). (2009). Absolute Generality. Cambridge, MA: The MIT Press.

Read, S. (1994). Formal and Material Consequence. Journal of Philosophical Logic, 23: 247–265.

Read, S. (2008). Harmony and Necessity. In C. Dégremont, L. Kieff, & H. Rückert (Eds.), Dialogues, Logics and Other Strong Things: Essays in honour of Shahid Rahman. London: College, pp. 285–303.

Read, S. (2010). General-Elimination Harmony and the Meaning of the Logical Constants. Journal of Philosophical Logic, 39: 557–576.

Read, S. (2019). Anti-Exceptionalism about Logic. Australasian Journal of Logic, 16(7): 298–318.

Richardson, A. (2023). Logical Empiricism. Cambridge: Cambridge University Press.

Ricketts, T. (1985). Frege, the Tractatus, and the Logocentric Predicament. Nous, 19: 3–15.

Rossberg, M., & Shapiro, S. (2021). Logic and Science: Science and Logic. Synthese, 199, 6429–6454.

Russell, B. (1918). Mysticism and Logic and Other Essays. Longmans, Green.

Russell, B. (1919). Introduction to Mathematical Philosophy, 2nd ed. London: George Allen and Unwin.

Russell, G. (2018). Deviance and Vice: Strength as a Theoretical Virtue in the Epistemology of Logic. Philosophy and Phenomenological Research, 99(3): 548–563.

Russell, G. (2020). Logic Isn't Normative. Inquiry: An Interdisciplinary Journal of Philosophy, 63(3–4), 371–388.

Russell, G., & Blake-Turner, C. (2023). Logical Pluralism. The Stanford Encyclopedia of Philosophy (Fall Ed.), Edward N. Zalta & Uri Nodelman (Eds.), https://plato.stanford.edu/archives/fall2023/entries/logical-pluralism/.

Ryle, G. (1954). Dilemmas: The Tarner Lectures 1953. Cambridge: Cambridge University Press.

Sagi, G. (2015). The Modal and Epistemic Arguments against the Invariance Criterion for Logical Terms. The Journal of Philosophy, 112: 159–167.

Sagi, G. (2022). Invariance Criteria as Meta-Constraints. Bulletin of Symbolic Logic, 28(1): 104–132.

Sagi, G. (2024). Logicality in Natural Language. Philosophical Studies, 181(5): 1067–1085.

Schilpp, P. A. (Ed.). (1963). The Philosophy of Rudolf Carnap. London: Open Court.

Shah, N., & Velleman, D. (2005). Doxastic Deliberation. Philosophical Review, 114(4): 497–534.

Shapiro, S. (2000). The Status of Logic. In C. Peacocke & P. Boghossian (Eds.), New Essays on the A Priori. Oxford: Oxford University Press, pp. 333–366.

Shapiro, S. (2006). Vagueness in Context. Oxford: Oxford University Press.

Shapiro, S. (2014). Varieties of Logic. Oxford: Oxford University Press.

Sher, G. (1991). *The Bounds of Logic: A Generalized Viewpoint*. MIT Press, Cambridge, MA.

Sher, G. (1996). Did Tarski Commit "Tarski's Fallacy"?. The Journal of Symbolic Logic, 61(2): 653–686.

Sher, G. (2016). Epistemic Friction. Oxford: Oxford University Press.

Sher, G. (2022). Logical Consequence. Cambridge: Cambridge University Press.

Sher, G. (2023a). Is Logic Exceptional? Universitas: Monthly Review of Philosophy and Culture: 23–41.

Sher, G. (2023b). Correspondence Pluralism. Synthese, 202(5): 1–24.

Sher, G. (Forthcoming). Logical Structuralism. In Ferrari, F. et al., Oxford Handbook of Philosophy of Logic. Oxford: Oxford University Press.

Smid, J. (2020). The Logic Behind Quine's Criterion of Ontological Commitment. European Journal of Philosophy, 28(3): 789–804.

Sober, E. (2002). What Is the Problem of Simplicity? In A. Zellner, H. A. Keuzenkamp, & M. McAleer (Eds.), Simplicity, Inference and Modelling: Keeping It Sophisticatedly Simple. Cambridge: Cambridge University Press, pp. 13–31.

Sober, E. (2015). Ockham's Razors: A User's Manual. Cambridge: Cambridge University Press.

Speitel, S. (forthcoming). Logical Constants. In F. Ferrari, E. Brendel, M. Carrara, et al. (Eds.), *The Oxford Handbook of Philosophy of Logic*.

Stairs A. (2016). Could Logic Be Empirical? The Putnam-Kripke Debate. In J. Chubb, A. Eskandarian, & V. Harizanov (Eds.), Logic and Algebraic Structures in Quantum Computing: Lecture Notes in Logic. Cambridge: Cambridge University Press, pp. 23–41.

Steinberger, F. (2009). Harmony and Logical Inferentialism. (PhD thesis, Cambridge University).

Steinberger, F. (2011). What Harmony Could and Could Not Be. Australasian Journal of Philosophy, 89: 617–639.

Striker, G. (2009). Aristotle: Prior Analytics (Book 1). Translated with an Introduction and Commentary by Gisela Striker. Oxford: Oxford University Press.

Tajer, D. (forthcoming). Logic, Reasoning, and Cognitive Science. In F. Ferrari, E. Brendel, M. Carrara, et al. (Eds.), The Oxford Handbook of Philosophy of Logic.

Tarski, A. (1936). On the Concept of Logical Consequence. In Tarski 1983, 409–420.

Tarski, A. (1983). Logic, Semantics, Metamathematics. 2nd ed. Trans. J. H. Woodger, ed. John Corcoran. Indianapolis: Hackett.

Tarski, A. (1986). What Are Logical Notions?, ed. by J. Corcoran. History and Philosophy of Logic, 7: 143–154.

Tennant, N. (1997). The Taming of the True. New York: Oxford University Press.

Tranchini, L. (2016). Proof-Theoretic Harmony: Towards an Intensional Account. Synthese, 198: 1145–1176.

van Fraassen, B. (1980). The Scientific Image. Oxford: Oxford University Press.

van Heijenoort, J. (1967). Logic as Calculus and Logic as Language. Synthese, 17: 324–330.

von Plato, J. (2014). From Axiomatic Logic to Natural Deduction. Studia Logica, 102(6): 1167–1184.

von Plato, J. (2018). The Development of Proof Theory. In E. N. Zalta (Ed.), The Stanford Encyclopedia of Philosophy (Winter Ed.). https://plato.stanford.edu/archives/win2018/entries/proof-theory-development/.

Warren, J. (2020). Shadows of Syntax. Oxford: Oxford University Press.

Warren, J. (2022). The a Priori without Magic. Cambridge: Cambridge University Press.

Wason, P. (1966). Reasoning. In B. Foss (Ed.), New Horizons in Psychology. London: Penguin Books, pp. 135–151.

Williamson, T. (2007). The Philosophy of Philosophy. Oxford: Oxford University Press.

Williamson, T. (2013). Modal Logic as Metaphysics. Oxford: Oxford University Press.

Williamson, T. (2014). Logic, Metalogic and Neutrality. Erkenntnis, 79(2): 211–231.

Williamson, T. (2017). Semantic Paradoxes and Abductive Methodology. In B. Armour-Garb (Ed.), Reflections on the Liar. Oxford: Oxford University Press, pp. 325–346.

References

Williamson, T. (2020). Suppose and Tell: The Semantics and Heuristics of Conditionals. Oxford: Oxford University Press.

Williamson, T. (forthcoming_1).Is Logic about Validity? to appear. In F. Ferrari, E. Brendel, M. Carrara et al. (Eds.), The Oxford Handbook of Philosophy of Logic. Oxford: Oxford University Press.

Williamson, T. (2024). Accepting a Logic, Accepting a Theory. In R. Birman & Y. Weiss (Eds.), Saul Kripke on Modal Logic. New York: Springer, pp. 409–433.

Wittgenstein, L. (1921). Logisch-Philosophische Abhandlung, In Annalen der Naturphilosophische, XIV (3/4), 1921; translated in 1922 by C. K. Ogden as Tractatus Logico-Philosophicus, London: Routledge & Kegan Paul.

Wittgenstein, L. (2009). Philosophical Investigation (4th ed.), Translated by G. E. M. Anscombe, P. M. S. Hacker, & Joachim Schulte, Revised 4th ed. by P. M. S. Hacker and Joachim Schulte (1st ed. 1953 Basic Blackwell), Oxford: Wyiley-Blackwell.

Woit, P. (2006). Not Even Wrong: The Failure of String Theory and the Search for Unity in Physical Law. New York: Basic Books.

Woods, J. (2014). Logical Indefinites. Logique Et Analyse – Special Issue Edited by Julien Murzi and Massimiliano Carrara 227: 277–307.

Wright, C. (1983). Frege's Conception of Numbers as Objects. Aberdeen: Aberdeen University Press.

Wright, C. (1986). Inventing Logical Necessity. In Jeremy Butterfield (Ed.), Language, Mind and Logic. Cambridge University Press, pp. 187–209.

Wright, C. (2021). Making Exceptions. Philosophical Topics, 49(2): 333–346.

Acknowledgment

Research for this book, along with open-access fees, was funded by the Stars@UniPD project CARR_STARS20_01 – "Abductive Methodology in the Philosophy of Logic" (AMPLog), led by Principal Investigator Filippo Ferrari under the supervision of Massimiliano Carrara. We extend our thanks to all the participants of the Euphilo Research Seminar (https://euphilo.net/) and the BoBoPa Research Seminar (https://bobopa.wordpress.com/), where earlier versions of some sections were presented. Special thanks go to Elke Brendel, Ole Hjortland, Ulf Hlobil, Ben Martin, Gil Sagi, Gila Sher, Sebastian Speitel, and Crispin Wright for their invaluable comments. We are also deeply grateful to Brad Armour-Garb and Fred Kroon for their great support.

Cambridge Elements =

Philosophy and Logic

Bradley Armour-Garb
SUNY Albany

Bradley Armour-Garb is chair and Professor of Philosophy at SUNY Albany. His books include *The Law of Non-Contradiction* (co-edited with Graham Priest and J. C. Beall, 2004), *Deflationary Truth* and *Deflationism and Paradox* (both co-edited with J. C. Beall, 2005), *Pretense and Pathology* (with James Woodbridge, Cambridge University Press, 2015), *Reflections on the Liar* (2017), and *Fictionalism in Philosophy* (co-edited with Fred Kroon, 2020).

Frederick Kroon
The University of Auckland

Frederick Kroon is Emeritus Professor of Philosophy at the University of Auckland. He has authored numerous papers in formal and philosophical logic, ethics, philosophy of language, and metaphysics, and is the author of *A Critical Introduction to Fictionalism* (with Stuart Brock and Jonathan McKeown-Green, 2018).

About the Series

This Cambridge Elements series provides an extensive overview of the many and varied connections between philosophy and logic. Distinguished authors provide an up-to-date summary of the results of current research in their fields and give their own take on what they believe are the most significant debates influencing research, drawing original conclusions.

Cambridge Elements

Philosophy and Logic

Elements in the Series

Classical First-Order Logic
Stewart Shapiro and Teresa Kouri Kissel

Logical Consequence
Gila Sher

Temporal Logics
Valentin Goranko

The Many Faces of Impossibility
Koji Tanaka and Alexander Sandgren

Relevance Logic
Shay Allen Logan

Propositional Quantifiers
Peter Fritz

Logic and Information
Edwin Mares

The Logic of Grounding
Fabrice Correia

Meinongianism
Maria Elisabeth Reicher

Free Logic: A Generalization
Greg Frost-Arnold

Probability and Inductive Logic
Antony Eagle

Logic and Science: An Exploration of Logical Anti-Exceptionalism
Filippo Ferrari and Massimiliano Carrara

A full series listing is available at: www.cambridge.org/EPL

For EU product safety concerns, contact us at Calle de José Abascal, 56–1°, 28003 Madrid, Spain or eugpsr@cambridge.org.

www.ingramcontent.com/pod-product-compliance
Lightning Source LLC
LaVergne TN
LVHW020350260326
834688LV00045B/1649